PENGUIN BOOKS

The Confessions of a Trivialist

BORN in Cleveland in 1912, Samuel Rosenberg has been a playwright, stage manager, play reader, university professor, photographer, lecturer, artist, director, scenarist, literary detective, war correspondent, and television producer and director. In the latter capacity, he created seven special prime-time programs, including *The Great Conversation* on worldwide ecumenism, *John XXIII: Pastor and Pilot,* and *The Forgotten Neighborhood* on urban renewal in Boston. Rosenberg is married and lives in New York. He is currently at work on a second book—a double biography of Sherlock Holmes and Arthur Conan Doyle.

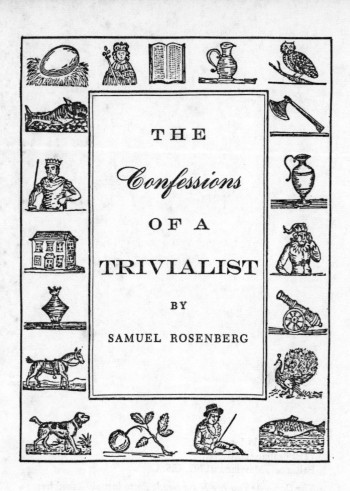

THE *Confessions* OF A TRIVIALIST

BY

SAMUEL ROSENBERG

PENGUIN BOOKS INC • BALTIMORE, MARYLAND

Penguin Books Inc
7110 Ambassador Road
Baltimore, Maryland 21207, U.S.A.

The Come As You Are Masquerade Party first published by Prentice-Hall, Inc. 1970. This expanded version published by Penguin Books Inc 1972

Printed in the United States of America by Kingsport Press, Inc.
Kingsport, Tennessee
Set in Linotype Caledonia
Typography by Martin Connell

To

my wife Angela

and daughter Ruth,

with love and gratitude

Contents

Foreword

THERE ARE probably many Sam Rosenbergs. I have heard of several. But there is only one "Sam" who physically fits his descriptive last name: "rosen berg—pink mountain," 300 pounds all around and six feet three inches high.

This same "Sam" also fits the "rosen berg" description metaphysically, for he is a whole range of pink mountains—pink in the twilight glows of brilliantly dawning imagination and brilliant conclusions.

So far as I am concerned there is only one *great* Sam, and fortunately for me that is my Sam Rosenberg, the philosopher, author, painter, photographer, raconteur. Our mutual friend Jim Fitzgibbon described Sam as being "probably history's most massive reader." Those of us who know him well realize that he remembers not only the main and secondary themes of *all* the books he has read, but also retains a vivid inventory of the myriad of trivia contained therein.

When scientists and mathematicians fail to find positive clues leading towards solutions of their problems, they sometimes reverse their frontal strategies and employ reductio ad absurdum, which by a process of eliminating all the *impossibles* and *improbables*, leaves a residue of *least absurd*, ergo *most plausible* solutions, which may be reduced, by physically testing to unequivocable answers.

Sam Rosenberg often resorts to these tactics by processing whole acres of trivia—significant details overlooked by others. By such a strategy he frequently has uncovered startling and heretofore unsuspected motivations of historical celebrities, and thereby reconstructed highly plausible but sometimes directly undocumented intimate episodes in the lives of notables.

Recognition of these episodes and their libidinous motivations often alters altogether the commonly held conceptions of historical characters. His reconstruction of the day-by-day and night-by-night conditioned reflexes, as well as the free thought processes of Byron, Shelley and their two ladies as they lived through the period when Mrs. Shelley was writing her *Frankenstein,* was so masterful as to win immediate publication in *Life* magazine. This story brought Hedley Donovan, *Life* and *Time*'s supreme editor, this reader's telegraphic reaction: "Byron and Shelley, belly to belly, belly good." And to Sam I telegraphed: "Your Frankenstein piece brilliant. Its language and strategy of disclosure constitute new era form breakthrough lyrical prose conceptioning."

For many years a top magazine photographer, Sam was asked to give a course in photography at one of the leading American universities. He would open his class by showing his students how to hold a camera and, after 60 seconds of such instruction, would launch into a lecture on James Joyce or some other of his favorite subjects. The students loved it and they learned how to get the really "best pictures."

Sam and his gazelle-like wife Angela have filled their home with the most extraordinary collection of once contemporary trivia anywhere extant. It consists of a galaxy of now admirable items that seemed too plain and "everyday" in their own day for anyone but

Sam to envisage them as worthy of inclusion in a serious art collection.

Living within that collection of profound trivia, Sam Rosenberg is stimulated to grow some of the most magnificent concepts to which I have ever been exposed. His mind grows out of environment like a giant redwood. He o'erwhelms me. He may well o'erwhelm you.

Buckminster Fuller

Introduction

MANY OF US are, I believe, the possessors of a cherished family anecdote, a romantic tale heard in childhood, or a talismanic book read during adolescence that seems to express perfectly one's sense of uniqueness, and that has even significantly influenced one's life. For me that special story, discovered in high school, is *The Pedlar of Swaffham*, a delightful "historie" written in 1699 by the 26-year-old Abraham de la Prymme:

> In Swaffham, in Norfolk, a certain pedlar dreamed that if he went to London Bridge, and stood there, he should hear joyous news. Afterwards his dream being doubled and trebled on him, he resolved to try the issue of it; and accordingly went to London, stood on the bridge three days, looking about, but heard nothing that might yield him any comfort.
>
> At last that a shopkeeper there, hardby, having noticed his fruitless standing, seeing that he neither sold any wares nor asked for alms, went to him and earnestly begged to know what he wanted there and what his business was.
>
> To which the pedlar honestly answered that he had dreamed that if he went to London and stood upon the bridge he should hear good news; at which the shopkeeper laughed heartily, asking him if he was such a fool to take such a long journey on such a silly errand.
>
> Then he added, "I'll tell these, country fellow, last night I dreamed I was in Swaffham, in Norfolk,

a place unknown to me, where methought behind a certain pedlar's house and under a great oak tree—if I digged I should find a great treasure.

"Now think you," says he, "that I am such a fool to take such a long voyage upon the instigation of a dream? Therefore, good fellow, learn wit from me, and go home and mind your business."

The pedlar went speedily home, and digged, found a prodigious treasure, with which he grew exceeding rich. Swaffham Church being for the most part fallen down, he set on workmen and rectified it most sumtuously.

And to this day is his statue therein, with his pack on his back and his dog at his heels. And his memory is also preserved by the same form in most of the taverns and almshouses unto this day."

Let others frighten themselves with the chilling tale of the man who fled frantically from Death to the distant city of Samarra—only to find death waiting for him at the city gate. I prefer the charming "historie" of the man who pursued his "impossible dream" and attained immortality in the stained-glass windows of taverns and poorhouses.

As I have read, reread, and proofread the various idea-dramatizations and unmaskings in this book I have been very surprised to discover how often I have stood on real or metaphorical bridges trying to emulate the Pedlar of Swaffham. So far no condescending shopkeeper has unwittingly given me the clue to a million-dollar (tax-free) dream; but I *have* received several bonuses of the kind prissily known as "treasures of the mind." They are not what I really long for, but they have been entertaining and encourage me to believe that one fine fantastic day a symbiotic dreamer will arrive to tell me his half of my dream. Or better yet, he may even wordlessly hand me a shining coin. I'll thank him, wait till he's out of sight, and then drop the coin into a magical slot machine that will instantly disgorge a great fortune in ancient gold coins.

A bridge experience: While working as a photographer in Italy, I was sent to Venice when most of the city was flooded by unprecedented winter rains. One night, after the waters had receded a bit, I decided to visit St. Mark's Square, but I never reached it, because a very dense fog swept in from the Adriatic and hid everything from view. Unable to find my way back to the hotel, I wandered through the deserted city until I reached the famous old Rialto Bridge (mentioned in *The Merchant of Venice*) and waited for someone to direct me. Finally an elderly man materialized, gravely listened to my problem and said: "The Hotel Danieli is a short distance from my shop. Perhaps you had better come with me or you will certainly become lost again in this fog."

Suddenly I remembered my "pedlar story" and realized that several of its conditions had just been met: a shopkeeper had come up to me on an historic bridge in a far-off city and had offered his help! Then another important Swaffhamite condition snapped into place when, as we walked along, I questioned him and learned that he was an antique dealer who specialized in Etruscan art—an exciting fact, for *all* Etruscan art is treasure trove found deeply buried in tombs or excavations. I eagerly anticipated the next turn of events.

As we reached his shop (he had come to check on possible water damage) he invited me in to see some artifacts brought to him "by some *contadini* [farmers] who had been indulging in a little clandestine archeology." One of the objects was a very beautiful large bronze *fibula* (pin or clasp resembling a modern safety pin) in the form of an embracing nude couple.

When I asked its price he replied: "Oh, it will probably go for about three hundred dollars, but I will hold off selling it for a long time. I want to keep it so that I can look at it and show it to friends and connoisseurs. Isn't it magnificent! It's from Tarquinia and early 6th century B.C. There are several like it in the Villa Giulia Museum in Rome. This type of *fibula* was worn by aristocratic Greek and Etruscan ladies to hold their robes together at the waist."

He opened the pin and held its sharp point close to his eyes. "The ancient myth tells us that Oedipus blinded himself with just such a pin he snatched from his mother's dress!"

When he discovered that I was an ardent Etruscophile who had made pilgrimages to all the principal sites—Cerveteri, Tarquinia and Volterra—and to the Etruscan Museums in Florence and Rome as well, he said: "Very good! You must see my friend's collection. His family has been collecting the Etruscans for more than a century—long before it was fashionable. You will be astonished. But first I must telephone that we are coming."

After a long walk through the fog-enshrouded city we reached the side entrance of a 16th century palazzo that fronted on one of the larger canals.

We were admitted by a venerable *majordomo* who seemed to have stepped right out of a classical play or grand opera. He wore a sleeveless candy-striped jacket, silk knee breeches, black stockings, and black buckled shoes. This most impressive (but slightly bowlegged) gent led us through a long corridor to an enormous library and museum filled with major Etruscan sculptures in stone and bronze. It was indeed an astonishing collection and richer, I thought, than any museum collection I had seen outside Italy.

After a few minutes we were joined by the collection's owner, a white-haired, elegant man in his late sixties who told me that most of the choicer works of art had been found on or near his family's estate near Florence.

As I continued to wander about the room, our host —whom the dealer addressed respectfully as "Excellency"—told the dealer that someone had recently offered him a "genuine painting by Tintoretto for only five hundred thousand lire [$100,000], including the cost of smuggling it out of the country for sale elsewhere."

His Excellency seemed to be highly amused by the offer and turning to me said, "When I asked this gentleman if it was really and truly a Tintoretto he answered with a long speech containing the beautiful word, 'Tintoretissimo!' By which he meant, of course, that the painting possessed Tintoretto's qualities to the ultimate degree of Tintoretto-ness. I almost paid him his price for that word alone. By the way, have you heard the story of the French millionaire who bought a painting by Correggio?"

When I shook my head, he continued: "The French collector bought it during the Fascisti days, paid a very large deposit, and following instructions, he went back to Marseilles to wait for the picture to be smuggled across the border.

"To get the picture out of Italy, the 'dealer' had a portrait of Mussolini painted over the Correggio, and it not only went through customs but was given a vigorous Fascist salute. When it reached the man in France, he immediately took it to his restorer to remove the portrait of Mussolini. But when the expert removed the picture he noticed that there was an *earlier* painting *under* the Correggio. With the new owner's permission he removed the Correggio and found another portrait—of Benito Mussolini!"

To be effective, "bridge-standing" must be done in far-off places. Nearly a year after the Venetian experience (1951) I spent several hours photographing the madly congested maritime traffic from the bridge that spans the Golden Horn Bay in Istanbul.

While waiting for a dilapidated ferryboat to arrive I sat on the stone balustrade of the bridge and learned from my old Baedeker travel guide that I was only a very short distance from the famed Bosphorus Straits, the swift-running channel connecting the Black Sea with the Sea of Marmora and the Mediterranean.

The travel book explained that here, very early in the mythological age, Io, the Greek maiden transformed into an ox, swam the then-unnamed Thracian strait from Asia to Europe while seeking to escape the gadfly that was stinging her to death. And *that*, wrote Herr Baedeker, was how the *Bos* (Ox) *phorus* (ford) got its name. (It also explains how American cows got the affectionate nickname of "*Bos*sie".)

Baedeker then placed the entire blame for Io's plight and frantic flight upon the King of the Gods, because Jupiter would not let mortal women alone.

The goddesses on Mt. Olympus were far more beautiful and infinitely more skilled in the art of lovemaking, but they bored Jupiter. Mortal women gave him greater satisfaction, and they were so grateful for his superhuman sexual prowess and staying power! One of those he seduced for his favorite Olympic sport was Io.

He was grappling with her in a secluded meadow

when, fearful of his omniscient, omnipresent and omni-suspicious wife Juno, he invented the smoke-screen—a great curtain of cumulus clouds around his outdoor bedroom.

The vigilant Juno guessed at once that the spectacular cloud formation hid her husband's latest infidelity and raced to the screen with ballistic speed. But before she was half-way through the protective barrier, Jupiter's super-natural radar sensed her imminent arrival and he instantly transformed Io into a heifer.

When Juno arrived she saw Jupiter standing in the meadow near the ox and pretending to gaze rapturously at the modest scenery. Juno wasted no time with preliminary dialogue and demanded: "*Who* is that?"

The divine Dagwood feigned husbandly surprise at the presence of the shivering and shaking animal and stalled for time: "Really, Juno, your grammar is deplorable. Shouldn't you be asking '*What* is that?' instead of '*Who* is that?' *That*, my dear, is a heifer, a female ox."

When Juno said coldly: "I want *that* beast. Do you mind if I take *it*?" Jupiter had no choice. "Mind? Why should I mind? You just run along home and I'll bring it later."

But Juno ignored his offer and whisked the metamorphosed Io to a palace dungeon to be guarded by the ferocious hundred-eyed Argus (he never slept) until she could decide what horrible punishment to inflict on her mortal rival.

Jupiter acted swiftly. He enlisted the aid of Mercury, who invented the flute and played a lullaby outside the dungeon where Io was captive. Soon the hundred eyes of Argus closed and Mercury ran off with Io. (Argus was demoted for allowing her to escape and is now a camera with only one eye.)

But before Jupiter could restore Io to her original shape, the enraged Juno set the murderous gadfly on Io and the epical worldwide chase ensued. After Io swam the Bosphorus and the Ionian Sea, she finally reached Egypt. Jupiter made his peace with Juno, the chase was called off, and Io remained in Egypt to become the goddess Isis.

Another and later "buried treasure" experience that may serve to explain the serendipitous nature of this book took place when I visited my friends Cynthia and Philip Mackie in Oxfordshire, England. Knowing of my passion for museums, Philip conducted me to Kelmscott House, the former residence of William Morris (1834–96), the highly versatile craftsman and painter. The ancient house and workshop was bequeathed by Morris to Oxford University and is now a museum of his work and that of his remarkable pre-Raphaelite associates, Dante Gabriel Rossetti, Edward Burne-Jones, Madox Brown and others.

As we were shown through the many rooms filled with furniture, wall coverings, paintings, Kelmscott Books, and memorabilia of the group, I noticed that our guide, an attractive and knowledgeable woman in her thirties, seemed to be rather abstracted. My attention then became divided as we continued to walk through the fascinating place, and soon she and the pre-Raphaelites were receiving equal time.

When the tour was over we thanked her and I (always eager to investigate unusual situations and the motivations of interesting people) said: "I think I know one of your secrets. You would like to become an archeologist and dig in places like the Far East."

She responded enthusiastically: "Oh, yes, I would. I'd like to do that more than anything else! But how did you guess that? Or did you? Have you been talking to someone who knows me? Or are you another Sherlock Holmes?"

"No, I'm not Sherlock Holmes. I noticed as you showed us through the house that you seemed to be preoccupied. You gave us an excellent guided tour but you also kept looking at the walls and touching them speculatively, as if there was something *behind* them. I recognized what you were doing because I share your obsession about hidden or buried treasure. It's a common idea, isn't it, that old houses like this have hidden rooms behind secret panels, secret Ali Baba caves in the basement with marvelous things in them?"

"But how does that relate to archeology in the Far East?"

"Well, as the man said, 'Elementary, my dear Watson.' I've observed that all of us buried treasure nuts are also fascinated with archeology, which is another expression of the same happy mania. The Far East? That was just a lucky guess."

She was indignant at this explanation. "Well, sir, it may be a 'mania,' as you call it, with you and other 'buried treasure nuts,' but not with me. There *are* things hidden away in secret rooms of this house. I haven't located them yet, but the original inventory mentions valuable things that have never been found. Of course they may have been disposed of by Morris, or taken by some of his friends or relatives after he died. Or stolen. But I've measured the rooms and palpated them and I'm convinced that some of these walls that are more than nine feet thick at the base conceal . . ."

As she continued with her long explanation I listened raptly for a time, but then both she and Phil (who had listened to our dialogue as if we were both stark raving mad) and the house faded out and a long-forgotten scene from my childhood in Cleveland, Ohio, played before me:

I was ten years old. I and two of my friends were standing under a huge buckeye tree discussing the sexual intercourse of adults. We'd learned about the mechanics of the fascinating but horrendous act from the pornographic booklets that circulated at Central Elementary and from photographs we had seen. But the question that stumped us was "How did the man ever get the woman to surrender to the bestial, degrading act?" Our reaction was based on our close study of the photographs that always showed the woman as dazed, bewildered and miserable-looking, like a defeated wrestler. As members of the age group that still believed that behind every wall there was a magical universe filled with treasure that could be reached with the right password, we suspected that men's conquest of women was also accomplished through magic.

Then Marvin Berger (the biggest cry-baby on the block) came up with the remarkable pre-Freudian inspiration that the man, the husband, the lover forced the woman to give up her greatest treasure by whispering "Open sesame!" into her ear. We approved the idea with mad enthusiasm, screamed a number of variations of "Open sesame!" and rolled on the ground ecstatically.

Then inspiration ran out and I looked about and saw a billboard over Kurlander's drugstore that advertised Bromo-Seltzer. "My turn! My turn!" I shouted and repeated the name three times.

Instantly, as if in response to the thrice-repeated incantation, a most remarkable thing happened. The front screendoor of the house across the street opened and the prettiest married woman in our neighborhood walked to her porchswing and began to swing back and forth most voluptuously.

We watched her in awestricken silence for some time, but when she made no aggressive move towards us, we held a whispered conference. Obviously the magical password had brought her out, but repetition was needed for verification and further development. And, since it had been my idea, I was elected to go much closer to her and repeat the incantation.

So, like a Western hero I walked slowly across the street to the epical showdown. I was petrified because we had recently devoted an entire panel discussion to some lurid stories of boys in far-off neighborhoods who had been seduced by vampire married women and *died of it!*

With wildly beating heart I finally reached the foot of her stairs, and when she glanced at me I shouted, "BROMO-SELTZER!" three times and then turned and ran all the way to 55th and Woodland, followed by my buddies.

End of preface. I hope these personal intellectual adventures have provided some clues to the character of this book and its author. If not, then I invite you to read what follows and suggest that you permit your own free associational memories to flash whenever they wish. Be my guest!

The Confessions Of a Trivialist

WHEN I WAS a boy, my father (Jacob S.) took me on a sight-seeing trip to Philadelphia. He was very patriotic, I remember. He named my brother William after President McKinley, and he always took his hat off when the flag passed by. Pa was totally blind, so we took turns nudging him when the flag was approaching and when it had passed. As a matter of fact, whenever we saw him standing in the living room, with his hand held reverently over his heart, we knew that he was listening to a patriotic song through the earphones of his crystal radio set, and we dropped our toys and stood stiffly at attention too.

Naturally, our first stop in Philadelphia was at Independence Hall, where we made the full tour. It was a happy and exciting visit for both of us, and we were thrilled to be on the very spot where our Great Heroes had Created our Nation. My father was most attracted to the Liberty Bell and "gazed" at it for a very long time. When I saw how deeply engrossed he was, I knew that he would be all right for a few minutes, and I slipped away from him to return to a glass case near the room where the Declaration of Independence had been signed—to stare in awe and wonder at President George Washington's false teeth.

They were carved from hippopotamus teeth and intricately fastened together with ingenious wooden dowels and bands of gold. The ivory was discolored by age, and the teeth seemed impossibly large, but simply because they had once been on such intimate terms with the Father of Our Country, they radiated a magical power for me that made all the other celebrated objects in Independence Hall seem impersonal.

I felt vaguely guilty though. I knew that I was expected to react to the various exhibits according to their approximate rank in the Scale of Historical Importance, and that my excessive interest in George Washington's teeth was not quite proper. But there they were, and I was captive.

Now, four decades later, in my swollen collection of Things, I have a copy of the newspaper advertisement placed by Dr. John Greenwood, the dentist who made the teeth, and also George Washington's somewhat muffled testimonial to Dr. Greenwood:

January, 6, 1799

Sir,
I ſhall alwayſ prefer your ſerviceſ to that of any other in the line of your preſent profeſſion.

Incidentally, if any reader wishes to see the charismagical Presidentures, he should know that they are no longer on display at Independence Hall. I have kept track of them through the years and can tell him that they belong to the Baltimore College of Dental Surgery and are now on permanent loan to the Smithsonian Institution. But it is unlikely that they will ever again be shown publicly. The teeth are in limbo. It seems that our days of innocence as a nation are over, and it has been decided that our new national image cannot survive the exhibition of such intimate talismanic hardware. But it is still possible to see them. I have been assured that for anyone personally escorted by the President of the United States the

Curator of the Smithsonian will instantly open the vault in which he keeps George Washington's teeth and let the visitor have a little peek at them.

The full realization that trivia holds a terrible fascination for me first came 25 years ago in Boston at the historic Old Howard Theater. The Old Howard had become a burlesque house by then, and now lovely Ann Corio was approaching the climax of her act; the pit band and the gents in the audience were urging her on with great enthusiasm. But I found myself glancing away from the stage to look at an "Exit" sign over the door nearest to my seat. I was enjoying the show and had no intention of leaving, but there was something about that "Exit" sign that intrigued me. It was made of old ruby-and-white leaded glass, and it glowed with serene quiet dignity in the midst of the commotion. The sign was about seventy years old, had originally been gaslit, and had then been converted to electricity at around the turn of the century.

For a very long minute I forgot where I was and stared raptly at the "Exit" sign as if it were a ruby set in the forehead of a temple goddess. Then I received the distinct impression that the sign was telling me that the Old Howard Theater had seen better days: "Once the words of William Shakespeare were heard from this stage—and Ben Jonson, and Henrik Ibsen, and George Bernard Shaw, Junius and Edwin and John Wilkes Booth, Joseph Jefferson and Jenny Lind played here to serious audiences. And," continued the name-dropping "Exit" sign, "Oliver Wendell Holmes and the James Brothers (Henry and William), and the Lowells and the Cabots, and Henry Thoreau—all sat in these seats."

When I realized that I was sitting in a seat that may

have been occupied by my hero Henry Thoreau, the great essayist who influenced Mahatma Gandhi and Martin Luther King and who had also, according to one biographer, invented raisin bread, I was stung out of my reverie and immediately recaptured by the charming erotic swindle on stage.

I quite forgot about that odd traumatic moment until a few years ago, when I returned to Boston to produce a documentary film about the rebuilding of the downtown area and saw wrecking crews tearing into the Old Howard Theater. Suddenly, with almost perfect recall, I remembered my experience at the theater. I entered the building and persuaded one of the wreckers to take down and sell me two of the "Exit" signs, and I took them back to my home in New York and placed them in my collection of Things. But I'm afraid they won't remain there much longer, because my wife wants to make a lamp out of them.

I have been collecting Things since 1930: surrealist and comic postcards, Sicilian wagon carvings, early broadsides and posters, rewards of merit for schoolchildren, tin toys, cigar-box labels, tickets of all kinds, glass signs of the Art Nouveau period, old match-box labels, defunct stock certificates (face value about $100,000!), and money from banks that failed during the Panic of 1837. I also have a few modern prints by Paul Klee, Max Ernst, and Henri Matisse, but most of my collection consists of graphic advertising art printed in America in the 1870s and 1880s. The artists who designed these pieces were among the best we had—Willard (famous for his painting "The Spirit of '76"), Frederic Remington, Maverick and others. Artists were not yet alienated from the general culture, and they created a minor renaissance in advertising art. They were proud to sell the products of the new

Industrial Revolution, to celebrate the phenomenal growth of the country, and they made thousands of little advertising cards for children's scrapbooks. My cards are cleverly conceived and brilliantly drawn, and they seem to offer a graphic calypso of the new America—a boisterous popular art form created by men of great talent.

It is a very heterogenous art collection. I select things for their artistic excellence or because they combine good design with a good story or with a hot cultural or poetic insight. Or simply because they are exquisitely trivial. Here are a few examples from my collection.

A faded blue card that reads: "U.S. Senate. Impeachment of the President. Admit the Bearer. April 8, 1868. Gallery. George T. Brown, Sergeant at Arms."

A Braille valentine. I have decided never to have the little goose pimples on this greeting card—it was sold to me as a valentine—translated, because the risk is too great. Either the message might be so poignant that it would break my heart, or it might prove to be so banal that it would destroy the unspoken poetry of the object.

An advertisement placed in a Raleigh, N.C., newspaper on June 24, 1824, by James Selby, a tailor. Mr. Selby offered a $10 reward "for the runaway Apprentice boys named William and Andrew Johnson . . .

about five feet 4 or 5 inches of height . . . the latter is very fleshy, freckled face, light hair, and fair complexion. . . . When they went away they were well clad—blue cloth coats, light colored homespun coats, and new hats, the maker's name in the crown of the hats is Theodore Clark. I will pay the above reward to any person who will deliver said Apprentices to me in Raleigh, or I will give the above reward for Andrew Johnson alone."

That Mr. Selby knew a winner when he saw one. But Andrew Johnson was never delivered. Instead, he opened his own tailor shop in Greenville, Tennessee, and Mr. Selby, discouraged, finally retired from business. Yes, the runaway apprentice tailor was the same Andrew Johnson who became the 17th President of the United States and faced impeachment proceedings in 1868.

A white-china plaque ordered by the Nazi High Command to honor the Germans' triumphant campaign in the Soviet Union, including the impending victory at Stalingrad. I was sent to Germany in 1946 to photograph the ruins of the German cities, the American Occupation, and the new Displaced-Persons (DP) camps set up for the survivors of the Nazi Holocaust. In the yard of the Rosenthal China Company at Selb, Bavaria, I saw thousands of these china victory placques, mostly shattered, being shoveled into refuse trucks. I found one that was unbroken for my collection.

A little slip of paper from Worcester, Massachusetts, dated July 26, 1786. It is a signed receipt recording the fact that a wagonload of hay brought to the weighing station of Thomas Lynde weighed 2,339 pounds. I bought this record of a commonplace transaction because I love early American printing. The early printers performed every job, no matter how small or humble, with great skill and pride in their work. As a result, almost any piece of paper that passed through their hands is worth having.

Also, by signing his name to this certificate, Thomas Lynde saved himself from total oblivion. Now, almost two hundred years after that wagonload of hay paused briefly to be weighed, Thomas Lynde is being remembered. His immortality is trifling and commensurate with the size of the transaction, but it is significant nonetheless.

A picture postcard of the 1920s that shows an elegant lady playing the violin in an empty cave. There is much more to this postcard than meets the eye. According to the printed caption, the lady is a "noted composer" who is actually involved in a serious artistic and scientific endeavor: She is playing a duet with stalactites that are resonating harmonically to the vibrant sonorities of her fiddle.

This item also happens to be a very good example of "camp." Some of the things I collect are very definitely in the camp category, but I must admit that I don't care for the word. It conjures up the image of a sophisticated and superficial consumer who regards the past as a kind of cultural smorgasbord from which he daintily picks little snacks to satisfy a jaded appetite. I believe in passionate, even fanatic involvement.

The people of the past did not live and create and die in order to provide material for our condenscension. Many of our ancestors, remote and immediate, were better people than we are and they produced things of greater quality. Who are we to condescend to anyone?

Each person who lived in the past had a full identity and was just as eager for love and respect as we are. When some of the creative-type "campists" reach for their scissors in order to cut up the work of the past for their clever collages, they are merely amusing themselves at the expense of their predecessors, who are no longer around to defend themselves.

But I have to admit it: A picture postcard of an elegant lady playing the violin in an empty cave is pretty ridiculous.

Stationery from the ill-fated passenger ship Lusitania. I will gladly swap some of my duplicates from the ill-fated *Lusitania* for similar items from the ill-fated *Titanic,* the ill-fated *Andrea Doria,* the ill-fated *Marie Celeste,* or any other similar disaster. I have always suffered from the compulsion to hear people say: "Gee-Wow!" and I have found that my piece of *Lusitania*na is a surefire "Gee-Wower!" For that reason I cherish it.

(Just as I wrote the word "cherish," my mind went sailing back to a time when I had just moved to California. Nervously I told my new neighbor, a fine gardener, that I had just seen a lizard in my garden, and she said: "You have a lizard in your garden? How wonderful! Cherish it!" What's the connection? Oh, yes. She kindly gave me a couple of bushels of compost to help my garden along, but she carefully picked all the worms that were in the stuff and put them back in her compost heap. When she noticed that I had noticed, she said: "I collect worms. They aerate the compost. I hope that you don't mind my collecting worms?"

I assured her that I didn't mind a bit and went home with my compost. When I reached my yard I noticed a robin redbreast with a worm in its beak. I quickly picked up the phone and told my neighbor what I had seen. "You're not missing any worms, are you?" My neighbor answered: "No, I don't think so. Please hold the phone while I look." The moral of this Proustian digression is twofold: First, some collections of squiggly trivia are very functional; second, when you give a wise guy some compost, be sure to give him the worms too.)

A broadside, printed in 1862, offering the services at stud of the celebrated young trotter George Patchen, Jr. Among the owners' stipulations: "He will serve only one mare a day. Positively none on the Sabbath."

A horseshoe and a sculpture of a Negro. Sometimes I buy things that repel me at first sight, that I really don't want, but that have some compelling inner quality that forces me to acquire them. I take them home and hide them, sometimes for months. Then I take them out and look at them, hoping to discover the source of their attraction.

I found two such objects in the same untidy thrift shop on a rural highway in Nebraska. One was a horseshoe in the shape of a woman's open legs. Judging from the style of the high-laced boots carefully engraved on the ends of the shoe, it was made in the 1880s. While looking at it one day, I noticed that it was not designed to be merely ornamental. It had actually been worn by a horse and was smooth on one side. Suddenly I understood. It was forged by a pioneer blacksmith who wanted to revenge himself against women (or did he have a particular woman in mind?). He had fastened those sexually open legs in the shape of a horseshoe to a horse's hoof and then had secretly enjoyed the sadistic image of a woman being pounded into the dust some tens of thousands of times.

The second object was probably made by the same craftsman. It is an uncouth but beautiful painted iron sculpture of a Negro servant who wears a high collar. When I bought this portrait head, I thought that the Negro was smiling (the painted image is not definite), but later, when I took it out of the drawer in which I keep objects with unresolved meanings, I saw that the Negro servant was not smiling at all—his head was raised in an attitude and expression of agony. I showed the piece to my wife and we speculated on its possible meaning. We turned it over and saw that it had been cut from a larger piece, that it had been the top of a hitching post. My wife said: "Of course he is in agony. They used to tie the horse's rope tightly around his neck!"

A collection of Italian votive jewelry, consisting of small locket reliquaries made of brass or plated silver. They are assemblages of cut-out lithographed figures, bits of gold tinsel, and other colored papers in which tiny fragments of the bones of various saints or other relics are artfully displayed and neatly identified. One little locket has a piece of the robe of St. Anthony of Padua (1195–1231), and another purports to contain a few threads from the veil of the Blessed Virgin Mary. They are fine miniature examples of peasant art, found in an antique shop in the old part of Naples.

I was taken there by my friend Peter Harndon, the architect and designer. Before we entered the shop, Peter said: "I know this bozo. He always manages to find really good folk art—and he is a true Neapolitan. I have seen him in action. Just ask him a question.

About anything. Anything at all. Then just stand back six feet and watch him rip."

As we came to the door of the shop, I saw the thin, haggard-looking dealer inside slumped in a chair. He resembled an unused marionette hanging limply from its guide strings. But the instant we crossed the threshold, the invisible strings had been pulled taut, and he was on his feet, alert, smiling, and attentive.

Peter was right. The dealer had some fascinating pieces of votive jewelry. The marked prices were reasonable, and we both decided to buy some. But I also wanted to see the dealer do his stuff, so I asked him: "Are they genuine? How old are they? What is their significance?" Then, following Peter's instructions, I stepped back two paces and waited for the answers.

The dealer began by looking at us very gravely. Then he picked up several pieces. "This one," he said, "is genuine. Also these two. If you open them up, you will find in each one a certificate of authenticity. This one, for example, is signed by the Archbishop of Ferrara, and is dated 1789. The genuine reliquaries are sold only to those people who promise to preserve them as they are. The others are spurious or homemade, and have no certificates. They were all made more than a hundred years ago, when the priests persuaded the peasants to give up wearing pagan relics and Roman phallic amulets. So the peasants threw away the *roba Romana* [Roman junk] and replaced them with Christian relics."

He put the things down. "But," he said, "before I answer your last question, may I, in turn, ask you which esteemed religions have the honor of including you two gentlemen in their memberships?"

"I am a Protestant," said Peter, "and my friend is a Hebrew."

The answer sent the dealer into raptures: "Protestant! Hebrew! Congratulations! How I envy anyone who belongs to a truly monotheistic religion! Each of you worships one God! A God who sits with great dignity alone in an uncluttered Heaven!"

Then, scornfully: "But we superstitious Italians are not content with one God! Yes, in principle we are monotheistic, but in practice we worship hundreds of saints. We have saints. We have Santa Anna, Santa Beatrice, Santa Caterina, Santa Diana!" As he joyfully intoned the names of the saints, he went into a spirited dance of genuflections, with his hands clasped in prayer and his legs executing a series of rapid deep knee bends. "We have Santa Eusapia, Santa Francesca, Santa Giuseppa, Santa Inez, Santa Juliana, Santa Margherita, Santa Lucia, Santa Ofelia."

He stopped for breath. "Those are just a few of the feminine saints, but we also have gentleman saints: Pietro, Marco, Giovanni, Hieronymo, Isidoro, Tomasso and saints et cetera, et cetera, et cetera!"

He looked at me. "You, sir, want to know the significance of these religious trifles, why the peasants wore them? Well, most people could not understand religion expressed in grand abstract terms. The common man needed to own a bit of the robe of a holy man, a piece of the shin-bone or forefinger of his favorite saint, or something that a sacred person had touched or blessed. He needed to hold God in his hand."

He gulped emotionally. "Excuse me, but I find that very moving."

Then he shook with anger: "But now! Now the modern Italian seems to have no need of such beautiful spiritual jewelry. Do you know, gentlemen, can you guess what the modern sophisticated Italian does with these sacred objects? He throws out the old Christian relics, and he replaces them with photographs of himself and his little baby. His own image! His baby's image! This is sacrilege! Madness! Egolatry! Bambinolatry!"

Peter Harndon and I had to restrain ourselves from applauding this brilliant commedia dell'arte improvisation. What a salesman! We bought all the votive pieces without even discussing the prices. Who would dare to haggle with such an artist? Later, when we left the shop, the dealer was still shaking his head sadly over the decline of spiritual values in the modern world, and the traveler's checks that he held loosely in his hand seemed mere dross.

When I returned to Rome, I became uneasy with my objects of veneration belonging to another religion and gave the genuine pieces of votive jewelry (those with tiny certificates of authentication tucked away in them) to Cleo Russo, a colleague in the Marshall Plan. She took them, thanked me, grabbed her coat, and raced out of the office. Later she explained why she had left so abruptly. "It was my lunch hour anyway, so I took the relics down to the American church to have them blessed by Father Sullivan. You see," she said sweetly, "they had been in infidel hands—yours! But I also lit a candle for you and your family for giving them to me."

A printed handbill advertising an "exhibition of left-handed penmanship executed by a soldier of the Confederacy who, unfortunately, lost his right hand at the Battle of Gettysburg." I have it framed together with a handbill published by the same organization that advertises an "exhibition of right-handed penmanship executed by a soldier of the Union Army who, unfortunately, lost his left hand at the battle of Gettysburg."

A ticket to a poorhouse in Buffalo, good for six months, 1864. Not a very inspired work of art. It is as drab as the life of the poor fellow who carried it. What gets me is the clause "for six months." There was no security or tenure in that poorhouse. The saddest of trivia.

A reserved-seat ticket for a movie house in a Displaced-Persons Camp near Hamburg, Germany. This camp housed a group of passengers who were forcibly removed from the illegal Jewish immigrant ship *Exodus* at Haifa, Palestine, in 1947. Earlier that year I traveled with and photographed 250 Jewish orphan children on a freight train from Munich to Marseilles. When I left the children, neither they nor I knew that they would be loaded onto the *Exodus* in a few days.

Nineteen years later I went to Israel, found some of the same little passengers from that train, and made a documentary film about them. One of the "children," now forty years old and with children of his own, gave me this long-saved memento of an hour's entertainment in the lives of a few survivors of the German extermination camps in Poland.

A blue-and-white ceramic mustard jar in the shape of Louis Blériot flying the English Channel in 1909. The mustard spoon, formed like the propellor of Blériot's monoplane, is alas, missing.

A petrified apple found in a coal mine in eastern Silesia, liberated by me after World War II. (I liberated the apple, not the coal mine.) Recently I was asked, "Is there a petrified worm in your apple?" I would like to have the answer to that question, but in order to find out I would have to destroy a piece of fruit millions of years old—a tough Solomonic judgment for a Trivialist to make.

Treasures! Treasures! Treasures! But in my present collection of some 5,500 Things I do have a favorite. It is a calling card that I found recently in a London bookshop. It is delicately—impressively—engraved with the name "Alanienouidet, Chief of the Huron Tribe of Indians." I found it pasted, together with several other calling cards, to a page torn from a Victorian family album.

All agog, I paid for my find (about $5), hurried back to my hotel, and plunged the album page into a basin filled with cold water. When the cards came away from their backing, I saw that there was a name printed on the back of the Indian chief's calling card: "Mr. Kean."

That same day I went to the reading room of the British Museum, where I lunged at the encyclopedias. I soon learned that my "Mr. Kean" undoubtedly was Edmund Kean, the great actor of the early nineteenth century. I read on and learned that in 1825 Kean had become involved in a sensational scandal and trial (Cox *v.* Kean).

It seems that for some years Kean had been intimate with the wife of Robert Albion Cox, a banker, gold refiner, and Alderman of the City of London. Suddenly Mr. Cox sued Kean for alienation of affections and for "criminal conversations." Several contemporary journals said plainly that Kean could not defend himself very well because he had been living in a cozy coxy *ménage à trois,* and that he was in trouble because he had refused, finally, to yield to the blackmailing demands of the Coxes for more and more money. Kean lost the lawsuit and was fined £800, an enormous amount of money in those days. His own wife left him, and his adoring public quickly turned against him.

When Kean dared to give a performance of *Richard III* at the Drury Lane Theater shortly after the trial ended, "his entrance on stage was greeted by the battle cry of a barbarian horde that lasted for three hours, and he was pelted with nuts, pieces of cake and a bottle of an offensive drug." Kean said afterward, with the endearing naïveté of actors, that he had anticipated trouble but had thought that if he appeared on stage riding a beautiful Arabian horse and dressed in elaborate new costume he would tranquilize and then enchant the mob. But the bloody barbarians only hooted at his fancy costumes and shouted a few extra obscenities at the Arabian horse.

Prevented from appearing in England, Kean fled to America. But when he arrived in New York he found that the news of his scandal had preceded him. The New York *Advertiser* led the attack: "Americans, do your duty! No manager should allow this lump of moral pollution to contaminate the boards. Every female must stay away from the theater and males hiss their indignation." Kean tried to work, but wherever he appeared American audiences drove him off the stage.

Finally he went to Canada, where he managed to regain some of his former success. Then, in Quebec, a remarkable thing happened. A tribe of Huron Indians, led by their chiefs—Tasawandahootei, Tsione, Teachsandaha, and Tsodhahaissen—came to see Kean in *Richard III*. The Hurons evidently loved Kean in the role of the malevolent nephew-drowning Richard, and they found no fault with his moral behavior, which was very similar to their own.

Later, in an impressive ceremony graced by the presence of a British captain in full naval dress, Edmund Kean was made an Indian chief and a blood brother of the Hurons.

The kindness of the Indians seems to have deranged the great tragedian. When he finally returned to England to resume his career (his fickle public welcomed him back as if nothing had ever happened), he was no longer a lowly actor driven into exile by an unworthy rabble. In his own mind Edmund Kean was a "Red Indian King," a monarch who had returned to claim his throne.

For years afterward Kean held court at his suite in the Hummums Hotel in Covent Garden dressed in the buffalo robes of the Hurons, a black horsehair wig on his head, his face painted, moccasins decorated with beads, leggings covered with porcupine quills, and a scalping knife stuck in his belt. Occasionally, he would shout blood-curdling Huron war cries in his great Shakespearean voice and advance ferociously on his terrified visitors with tomahawk in hand. Then, in a mood of self-pity, he talked about leaving England and the theater "to take up his abode with the Red Aborigines of North America."

He never did, of course. Instead he had an engraver print up a large batch of calling cards for him as "Alanienouidet, Chief of the Huron Tribe of Indians." (The Hurons were not the first American Indians to see a Shakespearean production. Two hundred years earlier, in 1616, a performance of *The Tempest* by the original company at the Globe Theater, was attended by Pocahontas. Her husband, Edward Rolfe, the Virginia planter, had taken her to England, where she created a sensation. She was presented at court and "was graciously used by Their Majesties," but King James exercised his divine right to be ridiculous by censuring Mr. Rolfe for presuming above his station to marry a "Princess."

Then, in another encounter, suggesting a dadaist collage of totally unrelated images, Pocahontas was visited one evening "by a vast man like a barrel, in a dirty brown cloak that dripped water. He was Ben Jonson and he was drunk." The great dramatist spoke to her for a few minutes and then seemed to lose interest, and "she crept away."

But in his play *Staple for News* (1625) Jonson wrote,

> The blessed Pocahontas, as the Historians call her,
> and a great King's daughter in Virginia,
> Hath been in the womb of a tavern.

In 1617 the unfortunate Pocahontas started for home, but, while her ship was anchored in the Thames among Sir Walter Raleigh's fleet waiting to accompany Raleigh part of the way on his ill-fated expedition to the Orinoco River in search of gold, Pocahontas contracted smallpox and died. She was buried in a churchyard in London.

For many years I kept my collection of Things, especially the trivial ones, a semisecret because it was so difficult for me to explain, even to my friends. Like most everyone else, I have some intellectual pretensions and like to be thought of as a man who keeps up with the major issues and the more fashionable ideas of his time. And here I was with an ever-growing number of very unfashionable trifles from the past.

However, recent developments have made it possible for me to come out into the open and safely admit my absorption. New York's Metropolitan Museum of Art, Oxford University, and several other such venerable institutions have acquired large collections of the most trivial things, so that collections like mine have been given some very classy, sophisticated-sounding names: "Camp," "Printed Ephemera," "Business Memorabilia," "Cultural Detritus," "Popular Art," and so on. This has given me some status and now when people ask me about my collection I quickly haul out one of the new fancy names.

But I find that, instead of feeling grateful for being made respectable at last, I am disturbed that great museums and universities have taken up this kind of collecting. How can things remain trivial when they are kept in mahogany cases (instead of in old shoe boxes under the bed) and surrounded with curators, armed guards, boards of trustees, burglar alarms, and closed-circuit television surveillance systems? Also, dammit, all of this is making the price of the stuff I buy go up!

There is some small comfort, however, in the thought that you can, if you wish, now go from the great masterpieces in the picture galleries at the Metropolitan Museum of Art to the Print Department Study room close by and there—by appointment only—can look at album after album of baseball bubble-gum cards. Yes, you can commute between Rembrandt and Bobby Feller, El Greco and Babe Ruth, Correggio and Casey Stengel, and between Giotto and Dizzy Dean. But I don't advise doing it all on the same day because it might give you a bad case of the bends.

Actually, there is nothing really new about such collections in an important museum of art. If you go through the galleries of the Louvre, the British Museum, or the Metropolitan Museum, you will find, in glass cases, large collections of objects from the daily lives of earlier civilizations. The cultural historian or archaeologist is just as interested in the trivialities of ancient life as he is in the great temples and the intellectual formulations carved on the facades of buildings. Together they give a complete picture of life in ancient days.

(Once a friend of mine took a group of small schoolchildren on a tour of the Egyptian rooms at the Metropolitan. They looked at cases filled with fascinating toys and cosmetic objects, and other Things. Suddenly one of the children shouted in alarm, "They're eating up the exhibit!" She pointed at one of the cases. Guards came running over. They discovered that streams of little black ants were marching to and from a piece of bread found in a tomb of the 18th Dynasty, jauntily carrying away bits of three-thousand-year-old bread. The case was immediately opened, the bread and ants whisked away, and a sign placed inside: "Removed for Repairs.")

The baseball cards at the Met are part of an enormous and beautiful collection of Printed Ephemera donated to the museum by a remarkable collector of Americana, Jefferson Burdick of New York. It includes many printed cards advertising the imminent departure in the 1850s, of the Yankee clipper ships that sailed to the California gold rush and to the East to bring back spices, tea, and coffee. The Burdick Collection, together with other similar Things that the museum assembled for years under the direction of its brilliant curator, A. Hyatt Mayor, is a first-rate repository of source materials for cultural historians and connoisseurs of graphic design.

Of course, Rembrandt, Dürer, Goya, Mantegna, Cézanne, Picasso, and the truly serious artists take precedence over the collection of vulgariana, which is only a very small part of the Met's general print collection. But one can spot a trend here: The line of division between serious and popular art is fast disappearing.

Did you know that part of the original manuscript of *The Importance of Being Earnest* by Oscar Wilde is in the Arents Tobacco Collections at the New York Public Library? When I asked the curator what it was doing in a collection of nicotiana, he told me that Mr. Arents bought the play script because the first act of *Importance* hinges on a cigarette case. What a brilliantly trivial thing to do!

But Oscar Wilde, certainly the greatest Trivialist of our century, topped Mr. Arents with a notation he made on the manuscript itself. Originally he had dedicated the play as "A trivial play for serious people," but the notation reverses the order of the words, and now it reads: "A serious play for trivial people."

I entered the present phase of my collecting in 1954, when I found, in an antique shop on Cape Cod, a scrapbook filled with advertising cards of the 1880s, valentines, rewards of merit for schoolchildren, and various tickets to county fairs and theaters. I was touched by the littleness, the anonymity, and the lack of presumption of the things in the scrapbook and decided that I wanted to collect them. But I had no idea where more might be found. In *Hobbies* magazine I saw the address of a man who wanted to buy some advertising cards of the period I was interested in.

I wrote to him and asked if I could visit him and see his collection, and a week later I was in his home. He had more than a million items in his collection, mostly picture postcards printed before 1915, and he showed me shoe box after shoe box filled with very interesting images of an America beyond recall: Steam Locomotives, Streetcars, horse-drawn Fire Engines, Suffragettes, Santa Clauses, and Pretty Girls. But he was quite evasive about showing me what I had come to see.

Finally, I asked, "Aren't you going to show me any advertising cards?" He replied, "No, I think that if I showed you the cards I wouldn't be doing you any favor."

I looked at him, rather stupidly I suppose, and asked, "Why?"

"Let me explain. You're a beginning collector of this material, right? Now, suppose I showed you what I have. There are about fifteen thousand first-class beauties in my collection—one of the best in America. Okay, you look at my collection. You say: 'Gee, there's a real beauty! And there's another one! And that one!' You'll want to buy some of them. But nothing in this house is for sale. You'll go away. Then, one day you'll see a collection of cards that are for sale. You'll look at them and you'll say: 'That's a *real beauty*, but I've got it. And there's another *real beauty* but I've got that one, too.' But," said the collector, looking me right in the eye, "you won't have the cards. You'll think you have them, because if I let you look at them now, *you'll steal them mentally!*"

I suppressed the impulse to let him have a "real beauty" right on the nose, mumbled my thanks, and left.

Now, as a result of that meeting, I also collect collectors. Most trivia collectors I have met are very reasonable and helpful men, and there are some whom I respect very much. Recently, at the Metropolitan Postcard Collectors Club of New York, I met an elderly man who has the world's largest known collection of cast-iron manhole covers.

He told me, a bit sadly, that the collection of the 200-pound manhole covers presents certain problems. For one thing, he has acquired a slight hernia from lifting and arranging his iron street sphincters. Also, his wife won't allow any of his treasures in the house, and he has to go to a lot over in Yonkers every Sunday to visit them. When I told him that I longed to collect old fire hydrants and that I had over 200 color slides of antique fire plugs and other street furniture in my collection, we became friends. As soon as I can manage it, I am going over to that lot in Yonkers to see some early American manhole covers.

One collector told me that during the last war he had been stationed near Cleveland, Ohio. He was never sent overseas and instead spent three years training intelligence officers. He used most of his furloughs and all his free time in the city dump and junkyards of Cleveland, plowing through great masses of discarded paper. With the help of some professional 'scavengers,' he found a considerable amount of early American Business Ephemera, some of it from companies that had been in business for almost 100 years. When the war was over, he returned to his home in New York with eight large crates of material, including a number of rare pamphlets and books. He organized an archive and is now a leading research consultant and librarian specializing in printed ephemera and Americana.

If it seems strange and repugnant to think about a

middle-class American rooting around in the city dump of an American city looking for the discarded documents of the past, my friend would answer that many hundreds of volunteers ought to join him in helping to rescue the enormous amounts of the American heritage that are thrown away every day—records of old businesses that recount the economic growth of the country, personal diaries, old advertising cards and brochures, theater programs and posters, old books and pamphlets, early newspapers and magazines, comic strips—in fact all those things that are part of the kitchen midden of our own civilization.

It's funny. If a man searches in the debris of his own contemporary culture, he is called a "scavenger" (or worse), but if he dons a pith helmet and goes off to the exotic East, or Middle East, or Central America with foundation money in his pocket, he is called an "archaeologist."

After all, what is the usual procedure in professional archaeology? The scholar decides to look for an ancient city—perhaps in the Middle East. He spends years combing through the literature that mentions the old city: Homer, Herodotus, Josephus, the Bible, and so on. Then he goes to the approximate city site, and what do you suppose he looks for? He looks for the millions of broken pottery pieces (shards) that indicate a kitchen midden—the city dump of the ancient city. Taking a dramatic stance, he points downward with his pipe and says, "Dig here!" In the strata below the surface, he is pointing in the hopes of finding the subsurface shards, the broken water jars and household utensils, the broken and discarded furniture, lost dated coins, discarded cosmetic jars, glass-bottle fragments, dice and children's games, graffiti, words scratched on clay fragments—all the things thrown out every day by the people who once inhabited the lost civilization now under study.

From all this cultural debris, a good archaeologist (with some Sherlock Holmes imagination) can deduce a great deal about the daily life of the vanished people. He can tell what they looked like, how they made their livings, how they amused themselves, what they thought about the big issues of their lives, who their enemies were; sometimes, if he is lucky, he can even reconstruct the events that led up to the final crisis and catastrophe that ended the life of the city: fire, conquest, or epidemic. Of course, the archaeologist dreams of finding the city walls that will lead him to wonderful works of art and buried treasures. But, in most cases, he is content with the less sensational discoveries dealing with man's past history.

Not too long ago I attended a kaffee klatsch with some fellow collectors. After the manner of our kind, we swapped and haggled, and everyone came away with a few goodies. My prizes were some fine engraved invitations to firemen's annual balls of the 1850s and a superb illustrated passenger's ticket for a Erie Canal barge, dated 1838.

The highlight of the evening was a story told to us by Dr. Lawrence Kurzrok, a leading obstetrician and gynecologist and a prodigious collector of printed ephemera. He is an authority on playing cards and has 8000 decks, some of which are more than 400 years old. Because I insisted on knowing, he told me quite modestly that he has more than 5 million pieces of rare paper in his collection.

Dr. Kurzrok showed us four albums of German cigarette cards. They were printed around the turn of the century and are very pretty examples of the German *art nouveau* style. These albums, we were told, were just a very small part of a collection he had just acquired.

Some time ago, he traveled to Berlin to see a dealer who had a large stock of rare cigarette and advertising cards of the 19th century. The doctor bought some things, but the dealer would not part with a number of cards the doctor wanted. He did promise, though, to come to a quick decision about selling them and to tell the doctor as soon as he did.

But history intervened—disputes between East Germany and West Germany, brink of war, threats of atomic holocaust, the Berlin Wall. Word did not come from the dealer in ephemera and Dr. Kurzrok's letters to him were not answered or returned. Still, he never gave up hope.

Then one day, during a thaw in the Cold War, a letter arrived from behind the Iron Curtain. It was from the widow of the dealer in Berlin. The family had moved to East Germany and was not allowed to return to the West. Before the dealer died, he had told his wife that he wanted Dr. Kurzrok to have his stock and personal collection. The letter concluded, "You can enter and leave East Germany, so please come and visit us soon, because I don't know what will happen." As soon as he could get away, Dr. Kurzrok flew to Berlin and eventually reached the town in East Germany where the woman lived.

He had never seen the entire stock and personal collection of the dealer, and it had been expanded considerably during the intervening years. The woman and her daughter kept pulling boxes and packages of cards from storage spaces and alcoves until the room, as big as an average American living room, was filled from wall to wall and from floor to ceiling—a total of two and a half tons of cigarette and trade cards!

Dr. Kurzrok did not hesitate. He bought the collection, had it packed, and found a shipper to take it to Hamburg, where it was to be put on a boat for the United States.

At the border between East and West Germany, the truck was stopped and subjected to a routine search. As luck would have it, the very first box opened by the *Ostgermanischengrenzwachtsoldaten* happened to be cigarette cards printed during the Nazi period. When the guards saw the faces of Hitler, Goebbels, and Goering on the cards, they immediately impounded the entire shipment, detained the driver of the truck, and put through a hurried call to the *Grenzwachtkommand.* The officers took another look at that box, realized that they had a *heise Kartoffel* (hot potato) on their hands, and sent the truck and its contents to East Berlin for examination by experts.

East German counterintelligence apparently could not believe that any American would go to so much trouble and expense just to bring out cigarette cards. Obviously, this whole thing was an extraordinary ruse designed as a decoy or front for some other big espionage move on the part of counterrevolutionary agents in the pay of the Western capitalistic aggressors. Months went by while East German men inspected every trifle in that vast collection of approximately 150,000 cards. (As they plowed patiently through sets of cards showing German Birds, German Flowers, German Heroes, German Automobiles, German Film Stars, German Scientists, German Rocks and Minerals, German Soldiers and their Uniforms, German Bombers of World Wars I and II did they sometimes recall innocent childhood days when they had owned some of the very same cards they were now examining for secret microdot messages?)

Finally, exhausted and still confused, they gave up, applied four official rubber stamps to every box—and shipped it all back to the woman who had sold it to Dr. Kurzrok!

In order to avoid a repetition of the border incident, Dr. Kurzrok had the two and half tons of ephemera flown to Hamburg and then sent to New York on a tramp steamer. Still quite ruffled and breathing heavily from its trying experiences, the collection that came in from the cold is now resting in a warehouse until its new owner can have it fully catalogued.

Frankenstein, Or Daddy's Little Monster

AT 1:00 IN THE MORNING some months ago, I drifted from my insomniac sack to the living room to play Television Russian Roulette. It is a mentally hazardous game but easy to play. Push the "ON" button of your electronic genie, bravely twirl the channel-selector, and then fatalistically watch whatever film materializes. If the little plastic wheel of fortune comes up with a test pattern or a hissing blank screen, you just twirl the knob until you find a program.

On that fateful night my reluctant old set warmed up, as it frequently does, with a brief lunatic survey of cubist art. First an ectoplasmal dot appeared, grew ominously larger and larger, and then silently exploded into an abstract painting, askew and distorted. Then dozens of crooked abstractions danced across the screen in a berserk video-frigmatic fandango and hurled themselves into a tiny black void. Finally, a bogus-looking Picasso appeared, glared at me, and leaped into that mysterious little black nothingness. The convulsive art exhibit ended abruptly, there was a suspenseful pause, and the film program began: *The Bride of Frankenstein* (1935).

I was delighted and relieved. My desperate little gamble had paid off handsomely. Many of the films shown to us "night people" are so crummy that not even hardened cinema historians can bear to watch them. They are chosen by stingy network misanthropes on the cruelly accurate assumption that anyone who sits in front of a television cyclops in the middle of the night will be grateful for anything shown.

But this. . . . *this* was producer-director James Whale's brilliant sequel to his 1931 classic, *Frankenstein,* with Boris Karloff; and probably the masterpiece among horror movies. So, with a couple of thousand calories within easy reach (somewhere in the world there is a marinated Silver Calorie with the name "Sam Rosenberg" engraved on it!), I settled down to admire the directorial skill of James Whale, Boris Karloff's superb pantomime, and the razor-sharp spoofing by Ernest Thesiger in the role of Dr. Praetorious, maddest of all "mad scientists." Dr. Praetorious, a pixilated but evil theoretician in the fictional world of monster designers, was added to the Frankenstein sequel for plot purposes: By threatening to report his "forbidden research" to the police, Praetorious is able to force the guilt-ridden Dr. Frankenstein to join him in manufacturing a "bride" for Frankenstein's misbegotten Monster, who has escaped and is inflicting his random homocidal vengeance upon society.

During the preliminary anthology of TV commercials—beer, bad-breath, cake mix, athlete's foot, dogfood, and hairspray—I had more than enough time to anticipate two sequences from *The Bride of Frankenstein* that demonstrate James Whale's unique genius for mixing chilling horror with Noel Coward-like comedy and satire.

The first scene, one of the most imaginative examples of gallows humor ever screened, is the initial meeting of the Monster and Dr. Praetorious. Dr. Frankenstein's horrible Monster has just eluded a pursuit of peasants and their sniffle-snaffle of bloodhounds and has found refuge in a deep underground crypt, in which some fairly presentable dead bodies are actually visible. Hidden in the shadows, the Monster sees Dr. Praetorious enter the crypt with two Quasimodo assistants, and he watches them angrily as they pry open coffins in search of spare parts for the female creature that Dr. Praetorious and Frankenstein are fabricating.

The fey Dr. Praetorious, who strongly resembles Jean Cocteau, shops daintily among the gruesome remains as if he is choosing diamond trinkets at Tiffany's. He quickly finds what he needs and airly dismisses his loathsome employees.

Left alone in the chamber of death (he is not aware of the Monster's menacing presence), Praetorious hums merrily as he opens a picnic hamper and gracefully sets a table on the lid of a coffin: a silver Liberace candlestick (he lights it), some neatly folded napkins, silver knives and forks, a few pieces of fine Limoges china, a small roast pheasant, a loaf of bread, and *two* exquisite crystal goblets and a decanter of wine.

Just as Praetorious begins to pour the wine, the terrible Monster and destroyer of men comes out of the shadows, snarling and poised to kill. But Dr. Praetorious, a creator of weird homunculi and a card-carrying ghoul, is not in the least frightened. He is *enchanted* by the creature's saucy display of strength and temperament and graciously invites him to join his cryptic, necrophilic picnic.

At first the Monster is taken aback by this unorthodox response to his ferocity, but he quickly realizes that he has met a human who *likes* him and smilingly accepts the invitation. That smile!

As Dr. Frankenstein's creation sits down, Dr. Praetorious gives him a rapid but tactful appraisal, rather as Gabrielle ("Coco") Chanel would look at a new cocktail gown designed by her rival, Elsa Schiaparelli. His quick professional eye rests for an instant, critically, on the Monster's haircut and the exposed electrodes in his neck, but on the whole he is favorably impressed with his colleague's handiwork and hands *it* a glass of wine.

Then, as he pours a little wine for himself, he winks flirtatiously, seductively at his guest and says, "This is my only weakness, you know!" At that the Monster gurgles happily. At last he has found someone who *appreciates* him, a friend.

The second sequence that I remembered was the stunning climax of the film. As a dramatic electrical storm rages above them, Drs. Praetorious and Frankenstein try to vitalize their female creature with great crackling bolts of lightning conducted into their operating amphitheater from enormous high-flying kites. (Storm? Lightning? Kites? Benjamin Franklinstein!) In a truly awesome moment their Promethean efforts succeed and the weird "bride" (Elsa Lanchester) comes slowly, jerkily to life.

But before the scientists can begin to educate her to her new duties, the Monster, awakened from his drugged sleep by the racket of her creation, sees Elsa, and in a spirited access of raunchiness seeks to begin his honeymoon right then and there. The somewhat flustered doctors finally persuade the bride to look at her hideous groom—and she screams in horror!

The unhappy Monster becomes so enraged at her reaction that he seizes the "Johnson bar" on the electrostator and pushes it over the red line to "full steam ahead." That, of course, sets off a chain reaction of tremendous implosions and detonations that destroy the Monster, his five-minute-old bride, and, regrettably, Dr. Praetorious. But at the very last second Dr. Frankenstein (Colin Clive) and his fiancée (played by Valerie Hobson) somehow manage to escape alive. Mr. Clive and Miss Hobson (now Mrs. John Profumo) are saved from that catastrophe, we now know, so that they may appear in later, similar horror melodramas.

Yes, a wonderful film, and I looked forward to seeing it again. The little bouquet of commercials ended with yet another humiliating setback for "Unruly Hair," and *The Bride of Frankenstein* began with a pseudo documentary prologue.

It is the year 1818 and "Lord Byron," "Percy Bysshe Shelley" and "Mary Shelley" are conversing elegantly about the great success of Mary Shelley's new horror novel *Frankenstein; or the Modern Prometheus.* As they talk, we are shown selected highlights from the first Karloff film, to sharpen our memory of the gruesome scenes: Dr. Frankenstein robbing graveyards to procure the bodies and vital organs he used in the manufacture of his Monster, the Monster's senseless killing of innocents, and his awful death by cremation while trapped in a windmill set afire by a mob of vengeful peasants.

"Lord Byron" performs his famous limp over to "Mary Shelley" and says, approximately: "It is a pity, my dear Mary, that you disposed of your Monster so utterly and irrevocably. The public are clamouring for a sequel." And "Mary" looks up from her embroidery and answers: "But, your Lordship, the Monster is *not* dead. He is alive and well, thank you; and I have just written a sequel for him, to be called *The Bride of Frankenstein.*"

I knew two things: that Mary Shelley, wife of the great poet, had indeed written the original *Franken-*

stein and that she had never written a sequel to it—*that* was a Hollywood fib. Suddenly I was intrigued by the image of the charming and shy young author presented by James Whale. Had Mary Shelley really been like that, so pretty and wholesome-looking? And if she was, out of what strange psychic cupboard had she taken the ingredients to create the most successful horror novel of all times? Where did that terrible yet touching Monster come from? Did her husband, Percy Bysshe Shelley, have anything to do with the writing of the book?

And then—most startling question of all!—had the devilish Whale deliberately used Elsa Lanchester to play both "Mary Shelley" and the Monster's "Bride" because he wanted to tell us that Mary Shelley had something in common with the dreadful creature of her imagination? (Unfortunately, Whale is no longer available for questioning: He was found dead in a Hollywood swimming pool in 1956, under mysterious circumstances.)

All of these speculations arose irresistibly from my years of experience as a "literary detective" for several motion-picture companies, which still sometimes call me in when they are sued for plagiarism. I help to decide whether there is a serious basis for such complaints by making analytical comparisons of the contending scripts; then, if necessary, I try to get my client off the hook by finding the literary antecedents of both properties. It is fascinating work, and I love to play at it occasionally by investigating the origins of creative ideas. Seated before my television set, my trained intuition told me that there had to be something very strange and remarkable in the story of pretty Mary Shelley and how she came to write about Frankenstein's Monster. I decided to search it out.

Now, after many months of intensive study, I have reconstructed, from more than thirty biographical sources, the chain of circumstances, events, and motivations that led to the creation of Dr. Frankenstein and his Monster. In so doing, I have uncovered a hidden drama in the lives of the Shelleys and Lord Byron and that in many respects it is just as unearthly as the fictional *Frankenstein* written by the 18-year-old Mary Shelley in close collaboration with Percy Bysshe Shelley.

Mary Shelley's book was only one of hundreds of "gothic novels" written in England between 1764 and about 1825. The genre was invented by Horace Walpole, the son of England's great Prime Minister under George II. Like Don Quixote, Horace Walpole felt completely alienated from his own century and preferred to spend most of his mental time in the "age of chivalry," residing in an elaborate plaster-and-wood imitation castle he constructed at Strawberry Hill, about 10 miles east of London. The building, never entirely finished, was a fantastic museum filled with good Gothic elements and flamboyant 18th century junk. William Beckford, Walpole's rival in building "follies" and writing horror novels, called Strawberry Hill "Walpole's Gothic mousetrap." When Walpole's friend, Lady Townshend, saw it for the first time, she exclaimed "Lord God! Jesus! What a house!"

But Walpole dearly loved Strawberry Hill and retired there (soon after his father's death) to spend his remaining 47 years living happily in a world of fantasy over which he was absolute monarch, and where his political enemies, literary critics, and all radical intellectuals screamed unheard in deep imaginary dungeons.

This dillettante antiquarian established the famous

Strawberry Hill Press, published hundreds of books, and wrote the letters that many critics have called "the best in the English language." In one of them, incidentally, he informed a friend named Nann that he had just (1754) invented a new word—serendipity—to describe the Walpolean behavior of the three fairy-tale Princes of Serendip (the ancient name of Ceylon) "who were always making discoveries, by accident or sagacity, of things they were not in quest of."

Early in June of 1764, exactly 54 years before the publication of *Frankenstein,* Walpole had a Ceylonese nightmare, from which he remembered only one powerful image: an enormous fist clad in armour, standing at the top of a great stairway. He immediately transcribed and elaborated his dream and published it on Christmas Eve of the same year as the very first horror novel, *The Castle of Otranto; a Gothic Novel.* It is a very rococo story about a ghostly ancestor who destroys his kin in a "sadistic farrago," and it delighted Walpole's readers. As only one example, a gigantic steel helmet crushes a nice little boy and at the end of the book pieces of the body of a great giant are found mysteriously strewn about the castle.

The Castle of Otranto was hardly noticed at first, but later, as the entire structure of European society began to fall apart at the time of the American and French Revolutions, dozens and then many hundreds of novels were written in imitation of Walpole's book. Oddly, significantly, it was the Marquis de Sade who first correctly described the genre and explained the reasons for the sudden epidemic success of supernatural novels at that particular moment in history. When the philosopher-maniac was not feverishly compiling his interminable scatalogues of imagined sexual depravity, he sometimes wrote clairvoyantly accurate diagnoses of contemporary literary and sociopolitical events. In his *Crimes d'Amour* (1800), written just before his final incarceration at Charenton (scene of Peter Weiss's play *Marat Sade*), the Marquis described the English Gothic novels "as the inevitable result of the revolutionary upheavals felt by all of Europe . . . answering the need for strong emotions following great social upheavals. . . ." In a brilliant phrase recalling the miserable social conditions of the eighteenth century, he added, "It was necessary to call hell to the rescue . . . and to find in the world of 'nightmare' images adequate to the history of man in this Iron Age." One of the most enduring of these therapeutic "nightmare" images was invented by Mary Shelley.

Mary Godwin (later Shelley) was the child of Mary Wollstonecraft and William Godwin, who were for a few years the most influential radicals in England. William Godwin published The Juvenile Library, for which he commissioned Charles and Mary Lamb to write their classic *Tales From Shakespeare* in 1807.

Godwin had achieved fame at the age of 37 as the author of the revolutionary *An Enquiry concerning Political Justice, and its Influence on General Virtue and Happiness.* Published in 1793, the complete two-volume edition has been out of print for more than 100 years but is still mentioned by scholars as a "great work" because of its influence on later social philosophers. Sir Herbert Read recently referred to *Political Justice* as "still alive, ingenious and profound, and . . . because of its tone of omniscience, finally boring."

The ideas in Godwin's nearly forgotten classic were drawn mainly from Voltaire, Diderot, and Thomas

Paine—and from the Jeffersonian ideals expressed in the Preamble and Bill of Rights of the U.S. Constitution: All men are created equal, and governments—"an unnecessary evil"—should exist only to bring equal opportunities and happiness to all men.

Godwin's book became the political manifesto of the English Jacobin "republicans," who were all close friends of Godwin: William Hazlitt, Samuel Taylor Coleridge, the Utopian Socialist Robert Owen, William Blake, Charles Lamb, the chemist Humphry Davy, and William Wordsworth. They believed in the democratic ideals of our American Revolution, and saw the French Revolution as a war of liberation waged by Science and Philosophy against the dark medieval forces of Superstition, Religion, and Monarchy. The Godwinians were convinced that the new experimental sciences were about to liberate all men from economic oppression and would soon usher in a beautiful moral epoch based on Reason and Love. The tenor of Godwinian thinking was expressed by the serious plans (later abandoned) made by his disciples Coleridge and Wordsworth to emigrate to America, where they planned a utopian philosophical-anarchist commune.

The Godwinian ideas were poison to the English upper classes, still in shock from the costly and humiliating defeat in North America and forced to look on helplessly at the slaughter of the French aristocracy in the Reign of Terror still raging only a few miles away. Unable to reach across the English Channel to rescue their friends or punish the guillotinists, they pounced instead on their own internal enemies. Some of Godwin's friends were tried for treason and imprisoned, but Godwin himself was never prosecuted. A Parliamentary committee headed by the younger William Pitt debated his case but let him off after it investigated and found that his *Political Justice* was so expensive (about $10) that no member of the impoverished lower classes could afford to buy and read it!

In all, Godwin wrote 28 very dull books on various subjects, including the brain-deadening "Essay on Sepulchres," but he could not be depended upon for dullness and also wrote two excellent Gothic horror novels: *Caleb Williams* in 1794 and *St. Leon* shortly afterward. Like Coleridge and other sophisticates who used the then-fashionable "Gothic" supernatural poems and novels as vehicles for their more serious, even subversive, ideas, Godwin skillfully loaded *Caleb Williams* with attacks on the evils of slavery, the injustices visited upon common people by those of great wealth, and his favorite philosophical-anarchist theme, more freedom for the individual and less for the state. *St. Leon* was another one of many contemporary novels dealing with the theme of eternal life and the curses that befall those who seek or attain it.

Mary Shelley's mother, the brilliant and dynamic Mary Wollstonecraft, was the daughter of a drunken, wife-beating Anglo-Irish farmer. She began her career in the only way possible for women educated above their class in the 1780s—as lady's companion and teacher-governess in the homes of the very wealthy. She soon switched to writing romantic novels, children's books (illustrated by William Blake), and articles for encyclopedias. She is remembered for her fiery feminist classic *Vindication of the Rights of Women,* published in 1792, when she was 33 years old. In it she declared passionately that the women of her time were merely the playthings of men, the phrase that became one of the sexier slogans of the international feminist movement and was later used by Henrik Ibsen, in 1879, as the theme of his *The Doll's House.*

After the Puritan Revolution of 1650, married women had absolutely no legal or property rights in England. The Church of England helped keep women in their places by dwelling constantly on their "natural inferiority" and sternly reminding them in the frequently quoted words of St. Paul, that they were still being punished for the apple incident in the Garden of Eden:

> Let women learn in silence with all subjugation. But I suffer not a woman to teach, or usurp authority over the man, but to be in silence. For Adam was first formed, then Eve. And Adam was not deceived, but the woman being deceived was in the transgression. Notwithstanding, she shall be saved in childbearing; if she continue in faith, charity, and holiness with sobriety. (Timothy 2:10–15)

But Englishmen felt that they needed more than biblical authority for protection from their encroaching females, and in 1770 (when Mary Wollstonecraft was 11 years old) the all-male Parliament actually passed a law that stated: "All women of whatever age, rank, profession, or degree, that shall seduce or betray into matrimony any of His Majesty's subjects by means of scent, paints, cosmetics, washes, artificial teeth, false hair, Spanish fly, iron stays, hoops, high-heeled shoes, or bolstered hips, shall incur the penalty of the law now in force against witchcraft and like misdemeanors, and that the marriage upon conviction shall stand null and void."*

* Quoted by Ralph M. Wardle in his *Mary Wollstonecraft.*

Mary Wollstonecraft's powerful attack on male supremacy and her arguments for decent education for women created an entertaining furore. She became a heroine to the liberal Godwinians, but the reactionary *Anti-Jacobin Review* described *The Rights of Women* as "a scripture, archly framed for propagating wh . . .s" and added poetically,

> Mary, verily, would wear the breeches,
> God help poor silly men from usurping b . . . . . s!

The attack ended with a personal slur upon Mary Wollstonecraft: "She's lent herself, O lovely piece! to half the town."

A few months after the publication of her book, Mary fell in love with the 51-year-old Henry Fuseli, William Blake's friend and like him a painter of powerful visionary images. Blake had very few friends, especially among artists, and he wrote an appreciative but confusing epigram for his friend:

> The only man that ever I knew
> Who did not make me almost spue
> Was Fuseli; who was both Turk and Jew.
> So, dear Christian friends, how do you do?

Fuseli, a gnomish man, was of course neither a Turk nor a Jew, but a former Swiss-German Lutheran minister. Mary had a special penchant for homely men of genius and, forgetting her own dictum—"nothing can more destroy peace of mind than platonic attachments. They are begun in false refinement, and frequently end in sorrow, if not in guilt"—she slyly offered herself to Mr. Fuseli as his "spiritual concubine." But Mrs. Fuseli knew a husband stealer when she saw one and kicked her out of the house.

Thwarted, Miss Wollstonecraft traveled clandestinely to Paris to witness and write about "the enthralling French Revolution." There, during the bloody Reign of Terror from 1792 to 1796, she formed a "free-love association" with an American, Captain Gilbert Imlay, a Western explorer, architect, and land speculator, and bore him an unlicensed child.

Mrs. Wollstonecraft, as she now called herself, refused to marry Imlay because she believed that "sexual intercourse must be free of social controls, and that men and women should remain together only as long as they love each other, and not a minute longer."

Later, in London, Captain Imlay found a new mistress and abruptly resigned from their association. Quoting Mary verbatim (the rat!) he told her that, though he was still in love with her theories about free love, he no longer loved her. Mary Wollstonecraft's biographers tell us that she responded to his superior and ungallant lovemanship by trying to drown herself in a "leap from the Putney Bridge into the Thames," but the voluminous, air-entrapping garments imposed on "men's playthings" by the morality of the time kept her afloat long enough to be rescued by some passing boatmen.

She was still slightly damp when she met, promptly went to bed with, and then agreed to marry William Godwin in April 1797. They were happy together, but their marriage ended in tragedy just six months later. In addition to her other theories, the 40-year-old feminist also believed in natural childbirth—unattended by male physicians. When they were finally called in, it was too late: Mary Wollstonecraft died ten days after giving birth to the future author of *Frankenstein.*

The bereaved Godwin gave the infant her mother's

name, a sort of "coldly remote affection," and quickly found a rather stupid stepmother for her. But from the start he made it clear to little Mary Wollstonecraft Godwin that she would have to atone for having caused her mother's death by replacing her intellectually. Godwin wrote in a letter, "I am anxious that she be brought up as a philosopher, even a cynic." Mary's half sister, Jane, added to the picture: "In our family, if you cannot write an epic poem, or a novel that by its originality knocks all other novels on the head, you are a despicable wretch not worth acknowledging.'"

As a small child the "solitary and withdrawn" Mary tried frantically to catch up with and surpass the ever-present ghost of her mother by reading voraciously and by constantly hanging about—an unnoticed eavesdropper—Coleridge, Blake, Lamb, and the other great intellectuals who regularly attended the Godwin salon. On one occasion, the Godwins were visited by the nefarious exile Aaron Burr, who recorded in his diary that he had heard Godwin's son William read a precocious essay on political science written by young Mary Godwin.

When Mary was 8, she and her slightly younger half-sister Jane Clairmont (who stage-managed and accompanied Mary in later scandals) sneaked out of their beds and hid behind a parlor sofa to hear the great Coleridge recite his immortal (and frightening) *The Rime of the Ancient Mariner*, the supernatural poem based on Godwin's axiom that "The death of love freezes the heart and causes endurable loneliness and destructiveness."

Godwin's remarkable eighteenth-century anticipation of Freud's basic explanation of emotional illness and delinquency became the central theme of the horror novel *Frankenstein* written only ten years later by the little girl who had hidden behind the sofa in her father's house, anxiously eavesdropping on illicit knowledge. Coleridge later commented on the "cadaverous silence of the Godwin children—to me quite catacombish."

The unfeeling relentless pressures on Mary in the "Godwin forcing house" (biographer Eileen Bigland's phrase) finally had their very weird effect. Mary Shelley never succeeded in matching the superior intellect and moral courage of her mother, and the incesant reading and writing under the cold shadow of her rival mother (she even attempted to finish stories left behind by Mary Wollstonecraft) served only to condition her permanently to associate books and writing with the "resurrection" of her dead mother.

Fanciful? When Mary was 17, she intuitively returned to the scene of the "crime" committed against her and began taking her books and writing materials to the nearby Old St. Pancras Church, where her parents had been married. There, seated in the graveyard behind the church, the haunted girl read and read and wrote and wrote under the willow tree that drooped mournfully over her mother's grave.

While Mary held her daily séances in the graveyard and grimly Indian-wrestled with the spirit of her mother, her father was losing his more worldly struggle for survival. By 1814 his former friends and disciples, who had naïvely expected Robespierre and Danton to install an instant Earthly Paradise in France, had long since become disillusioned by the new despotism that had replaced the old one. Coleridge and the rest had abandoned their liberalism to join forces with their old Tory enemies in fighting the French Revolutionists and then Napoleon. The deserted and aging Godwin was passé, his own books no longer sold, and his publishing business was on the verge of bankruptcy. But then he remembered young Percy Bysshe Shelley and put a desperately improvised scheme into action.

Two years before (1812), he had received an hysterical letter from the 20-year-old poet. Shelley presented himself as a "lover of mankind" who was being persecuted for his radical views, most of which he had learned from reading Godwin's *Political Justice.* He had modestly referred to his own writings but had not mentioned that he was almost finished with his first important poem, *Queen Mab,* published in 1813. He offered himself as a disciple and naïvely concluded his letter with the information that he was the heir to an estate that would bring him an annual cash income of £6,000 ($30,000) when his grandfather and his father died.

Godwin, of course, had checked on his panting young admirer and learned that he was a future baronet and the heir to landed estates in Sussex worth the modern equivalent of about ten million dollars. He had also learned that Shelley was already known in English society as an eccentric genius and rebel. The poet Thomas Love Peacock, Shelley's friend, described him as "like a small kingdom in a constant state of insurrection," a description that was later applied, word for word, by Mary Shelley to Dr. Victor Frankenstein, whom she based partly on Percy Shelley.

In 1802, at the age of 10, Shelley had been thrown into Syon House Academy, near London, one of those early 19th-century "Marat Sade" English boarding schools about which so much has been written. Years later a schoolmate clearly remembered, "Shelley was like a girl, dressed in boy's clothing, fighting with open hands like a girl, and rolling around on the floor when he was flogged, not from pain, but from the indignity." Intellectually far superior and even then a total nonconformist, he was soon beaten up by almost every boy in the school while the teachers looked on approvingly—a humiliation that Shelley never forgave. It turned him into the bitter enemy of his own social caste.

At Syon House and later at Eton (from ages 12 to 17) "Mad Shelley the Atheist" had seriously planned to become a research chemist or alchemist. He had discovered the wonders of chemistry and physics from the "magical" lectures of Adam Walker, 80-year-old apostle of the new experimental sciences. For five years, under Walker's spell, Shelley was deeply engrossed in the rationalist scientific ideas of Joseph Priestley, Humphry Davy, and especially "Dr. Benjamin Franklin," whom he regarded as the modern Prometheus, who stole God's lightning in order to bestow its practical wonders upon mankind. And, like the student "Victor Frankenstein" in Mary Shelley's novel, Percy Shelley gave equal time to the medieval occult philosophers: Paracelsus of Ingolstadt, Albertus Magnus and Cornelius Agrippa, who dreamed, as the young Etonian did, of finding the secret of eternal life.

As one learns all these things about Shelley, boy Promethean, it becomes quite clear that he must have been the model for his wife's fictional Dr. Frankenstein, the ill-fated chemist who fumbled disastrously with the secret of biological immortality.

The strong resemblance of Dr. Frankenstein to Percy Shelley is underscored by Mrs. Shelley's use of Adam Walker as the basis for Professor Waldman,

Frankenstein's teacher at the University of Ingolstadt. It is the kindly Waldman (the name Waldman contains most of the letters in the name Adam Walker) who "decided the future destiny of his young student" by turning him toward esoteric research in organic chemistry, which results in Dr. Frankenstein's discovery of the "secrets of life" and his resurrection of some dead bodies in the abortive form of the Monster.

Shelley had actually bought chemicals and equipment from Adam Walker's assistant and had performed a number of clumsy experiments that had caused dangerous explosions at Eton (and later at Oxford); nearly poisoned himself, and almost electrocuted an oppressive Etonian tutor. The 13-year-old "scientist" also tried to cure the lowly chilblain with an "electrifying machine," and, still obsessed with the Franklin-Prometheus image (his masterpiece is, of course, *Prometheus Unbound*), he personally challenged God by flying a kite during a severe electrical storm at Eton. God did nothing about his presumption at the time, but during a similar storm in the Italian Gulf of Spezia in 1822 He roughly gathered up the 29-year-old poet. (Characteristically, the suicide-prone Shelley ignored the shouted warnings of professional mariners and—blithe spirit!—sailed his little boat *Ariel*, formerly *Don Juan*, out of the security of Livorno harbor directly into the maw of the black squall.)

At 18, Shelley and his friend Thomas Jefferson Hogg were expelled from Oxford University after having published Shelley's unsigned essay "The Necessity for Atheism" (1811), in which Shelley asked for a discussion of the question of God's existence, and concluded: "Every reflecting mind must allow that there is no proof for the existence of the Deity.

Q.E.D." The exalted Master of Oxford University, not disposed to debate the question of the existence of the Almighty with the schoolboy Faustus who reeked of sulfur and shuffled about without laces in his shoes, ordered all copies of the blasphemous pamphlet burned and then tried to force Shelley to affirm or deny his authorship. Shelley refused and was "sent down" for impiety and for defending his right to free speech.

Shelley, an unorthodox atheist, professed not to believe in God but was definitely convinced of a hereafter swarming with ghosts, monsters, and devils. He slept on coffins in a cemetery charnel house near his home during one of his holidays from Oxford "to hold high talk with the dead" (or said he did); and wrote two novels filled with all the stock machinery of gothic horror novels: haunted castles, the Wandering Jew (before Prometheus, his favorite character), incestuous lads and maidens, bluebeard nobility, torture dungeons, and crazy Satanic Monks.

Shelley's first novel *Zastrozzi* (1810), published at Oxford when he was 18 but written a year earlier, is a high-spirited schoolboy parody of Charlotte Dacre's *Zafloya* (1806) and of several novels written by the brilliant erotic terrormongering Matthew Gregory ("Monk") Lewis, the Truman Capote of his century. Zastrozzi is a highwayman possessed by the devil; he seriously neglects his highway to devote his energies to his Monte Cristo search for Verrezzi, betrayer of his beloved mother, Olivia. Not only has Verrezzi ruined his innocent Olivia but also, when, pregnant and starving, she once begged him for a little pasta, he coolly suggested that she should earn her living as a prostitute. After a maniacal 24-year search, Zastrozzi locates Verrezzi, confronts him with his crime, and stabs him fatally. The naughty young Shelley let Verrezzi die in total bewilderment, being unable—for the life of him—to remember ever having met anyone named Olivia! After fulfilling his mission of revenge (maybe), Zastrozzi is taken to a franchised torture salon of the Inquisition. He dies bravely, "with a smile of disdainful scorn on his soul-illumined countenance; and with a wild convulsive laugh of exulting revenge."

St. Irvyne: or the Rosicrucian, Shelley's second novel, was directly influenced by Godwin's *St. Leon* (1799), another Wandering Jew-curse-of-eternal-life story. Shelley's young hero Wolfstein, a noble brigand, is almost persuaded by Ginotti, the unhappy possessor of eternal life, to take over his burden. But Wolfstein cops out at the last minute, and both he and the accursed Ginotti are destroyed by God's lightning. The name Frankenstein is, I believe, a combination of Franklin and Wolfstein, Promethean electricity plus the search for eternal life equal Frankenstein!

Shelley was also an advanced hypochondriac. Once while riding in a stagecoach soon after he had left Oxford, he sat opposite a woman with very fat legs and became convinced that he had caught elephantiasis from her. He constantly dosed himself from a bottle of opium he carried in his pocket. He was afflicted with frequent "violent seizures," which some unkind modern biographers have demoted to "temper tantrums." Sometimes his persecution mania led him to hallucinate that he was being homocidally attacked.

Two years after his humiliating fiasco at Oxford, Shelley, at 20, married Harriet Westbrook—against his family's wishes, of course—and then took his friend Hogg along on their honeymoon. With Shelley's tacit approval, Hogg tried to persuade Harriet to accept him as her lover, but Harriet refused and brought her sister Eliza into their home in order to forestall the triangular love ideas of Hogg and Shelley.

Later, when Harriet ignored Shelley's new-fangled "scientific" heresy—that upper-class women should breast-feed their own children—and hired a wet nurse for their first child, Shelley hysterically snatched little Ianthe from the nurse's breast and, according to Peacock, an astonished and convulsed witness, "he seriously endeavoured to suckle the infant at his own breast."

After shrewdly evaluating the biographical data that he had assembled, Godwin immediately began to cultivate "Mad Shelley." He wrote him long letters filled with disinterested-sounding Polonian advice and soon assumed the role of "guru" to the young poet and future millionaire, who was still racing madly about, tilting at windmills and squandering his money.

Finally, in 1814, the desperate Godwin made his move. He located the elusive Shelley at his latest residence in a remote village in Wales and sent him an urgent letter explaining his impending bankruptcy. He told Shelley to stop wasting his money on "lost causes" (like Irish emancipation and financial aid to former Godwinians still in prison) and come to the aid of Godwin, his intellectual mentor.

Shelley left Harriet, who was pregnant again, in the country and galloped to Godwin's side. Although he was already deeply in hock to money lenders and reduced to sneaking out of back doors to evade arrest for debt, Shelley managed to borrow additional large amounts against his future inheritance, at the usurious rate of 400%. He turned this money over to Godwin. All told, during the next seven years, the "venerable horse-leech Godwin" took Shelley for a total of £24,-

500, equal in modern values to about a quarter of a million dollars. (Yet immediately after Shelley died Godwin went into bankruptcy.)

During the first of these insanely impractical loan negotiations Shelley took all his meals with the Godwins, discussed Greek philosophy and literature (never vulgar economics), and became very aware of the beautiful and intelligent Mary, now 17, who sat with Shelley and her father. Mary listened silently to their brilliant discussions, fell in love, exchanged furtive hot glances with Shelley, and coldly planned to steal the highly gullible young aristocrat from his wife.

When Shelley noticed (as he was meant to) that Mary mysteriously disappeared for a time every day, it was Mary's accomplice, Jane Clairmont, who "volunteered" to lead him to Mary in the secluded Old St. Pancras graveyard and then "discreetly withdrew" leaving them alone among the tombstones.

The profound, infantile, death-obsessed, disaster-prone young genius and *shlemiel* took a longer look at the psychedelicious reincarnation of Mary Wollstonecraft seated by her mother's grave, and fell madly in love.

At first, the overwhelmed Shelley later alibied, he did not declare his love for Mary because of his deep concern for Harriet, then expecting his second child. But when Mary, who had inherited a bold trick or two from her mother, Wollstonecraftily declared *her* love, he was hooked. There, at once, in that gruesome Garden of Eden stage setting, Percy Shelley and Mary Godwin began their Adam and Eve improvisations of *Paradise Lost* and *Babes in the Woods* that later became an essential part of *Frankenstein; or The Modern Prometheus.*

Eleven months later Mary was mildly indisposed. "Dr. Percy Shelley," who was extremely perceptive in his saner intervals, wrote the following "comic" prescription for his ailing "soul-mate" in her journal (May 9, 1815): "9 drops of human blood, 7 grains of gunpowder, ½ oz. of putrefied brain, 13 mashed grave worms."

Perhaps the most remarkable clue to the personality of this juvenile monster-creator can be seen in the recently published private journal of Mary Shelley's closest friend and constant companion, Jane Clairmont, who wrote:

> Recalling her conduct in Pisa [about 5 years after the publication of *Frankenstein*] I can never help feeling horror even in only looking at her—the instant she appears I feel, not as if I had blood in my veins, but in its stead the sickening crawling motion of the Death Worm.
>
> What would one say of a Woman . . . how would one feel towards her who should go and gaze upon the spectacle of a Child led to the scaffold. One would turn from her in horror—yet she did so, she looked cooly on, rejoiced in the comfortable place she had got in the shew, chatted with her neighbors, never winced once during the exhibition; and, when it was all over, went up and claimed acquaintance with the executioner and shook hands with him.

Here, in a letter to a close friend, is Godwin's version of what happened during that first necropolitan rendezvous:

> On Sunday, June 26th, 1814, Shelley accompanied Mary and her sister Jane to the tomb of Mary's mother and there, it seems, the impious idea occurred to him of seducing her, playing the traitor to me, and deserting his wife. On Wednesday, the 6th of July, the transaction of my loan was completed;

> and on that evening he had the madness to disclose his plans to me, and to ask my consent. I expostulated with him with all the force of which I was master, and with so much effect that he promised to give up his licentious love and return to virtue.

But Shelley reneged on his promise. Like Captain Gilbert Imlay before him, Shelley (the rat!) quoted verbatim to Godwin the words of the departed Mary Wollstonecraft: "Sexual intercourse must be free from social controls, and men and women should remain together only as long as they love each other." Outfoxed, the nearly apoplectic Godwin accepted a large loan from Shelley, and Percy and Mary moved into temporary lodgings. There followed a brief interval of hysterical confrontations, in which Shelley tried to form a *ménage à trois* with Mary Wollstonecraft Godwin as a "spiritual concubine" (furiously rejected by Harriet), suggested mutual hara-kari to Mary (tenderly refused by Mary), and then dramatically attempted suicide with a massive underdose of opium. After these brilliantly performed token gestures of conciliation and expiation, the young lovers ran away to the Continent with Jane Clairmont, only to return after a few weeks and settle down uneasily in a house near the Godwins. A daughter was born almost nine months after their mutual seduction in the Old St. Pancras cemetery, but she died soon after birth.

The writing of *Frankenstein,* two years later, was the accidental by-product of the long "enchanted summer" of 1816, which Shelley and Mary spent in Switzerland in the company of sister Jane, Lord Byron, and the latter's personal physician in attendance, John Polidori. The lovers had wanted to escape Godwin's hypo-critical rages directed at their "free love" union and his constant demands for more money.

They also wanted to flee the importunate reproaches of Harriet Shelley and her two children. Harriet clung to her pathetic hope that Shelley—whom she now called "a vampire"—would realize how completely he had been swindled by the Godwins, living and dead, and return to her. (She gave up finally in December 1816 and drowned herself in the Serpentine Pond in London's Hyde Park, very close to the spot where the grownup Percy Shelley frequently stopped to indulge his compulsive and prophetic hobby of sailing little paper boats.)

Originally Shelley had decided to run away and take up permanent residence in Italy. He went to Switzerland instead because Mary and Jane Clairmont, who had grandly renamed herself "Claire Clairmont, the actress," once again manipulated and sidetracked him. Shelley did not know that Jane had been secretly intimate with Lord Byron in London, was now pregnant by him, and anxious to corral him in Switzerland. This time the Machiavellian sisters used the old gambit of double flattery on the two poets, and they agreed to meet for the first time in Geneva. The stage was set for the final act in the creation of Dr. Victor Frankenstein and his Monster.

When the Shelleys arrived in Geneva at the end of May 1816 with their infant son William and "Madame Claire Clairmont," they found that their scandal had preceded them: The story gleefully spread by English tourists that the "aristocratic renegade" Shelley had purchased the two beautiful daughters of godless Godwin for £1,500 (£800 for Mary, £700 for Claire) and was now living with them in a Pasha-like state of alternating binomial hanky-panky.

But, when the "infamous" Lord Byron suddenly appeared in Geneva a few days later in the company of the handsome young Dr. Polidori (whom he called Polly-Dolly) and moved into the Hôtel d'Angleterre, already occupied by Shelley and his bartered brides, the sexual arithmetic in the minds of Geneva's gossips became higher mathematics.

Byron's scandal was far greater than that of the Shelleys. After several years of the most spectacular literary, social, and amorous successes, the 26-year-old Byron had suddenly been ostracized by English society and viciously attacked in the London press as a Nero, Caligula, Heliogabalus, and Henry, the Eighth. Five months before (January 1816), after a marriage that lasted only one year, he had separated from Annabella Byron and their infant daughter, Augusta Ada. Annabella then told her friends—who told everyone else—that, beside being "brutal and mad" in his conduct toward her, Byron had repeatedly boasted to her of his homosexual affairs and was committing incest with his half-sister, Augusta Leigh.

Byron haughtily refused to comment on his wife's accusations (privately he pleaded "temporary insanity" for having confided in her) and exiled himself from England, for the last eight years of his life, first to Switzerland and Italy and then to Greece, where he died of a fever in 1824.

Now every brassbound telescope in Geneva was sharply focused on the doors and windows of the Hôtel d'Angleterre, and its servants were bribed for any lascivious tidbit they could report or invent about the scandalous troupe. To get away from all this goggle-eyed attention, Shelley and Byron rented adjacent villas on the perimeter of Geneva and settled down for the long summer.

Mary Shelley's terse and secretive journal tells us that the summer of 1816 was exceptionally rainy and dreary, and forced the young social outcasts to spend a great deal of their time indoors.

Byron and Shelley quickly formed an advanced seminar in poetry and philosophy and read aloud and discussed an enormous number of books, all dutifully listed in the journals of Mary Shelley. Mary, Polly-Dolly, and Claire (who, though witty and intelligent, was along only for the hay rides) listened in awe to the two great young poets. In those few weeks in Switzerland a miniature renaissance emerged that resulted in a number of enduring works, including Shelley's "Hymn to Intellectual Beauty" and the germinal concept of his great *Prometheus Unbound,* Byron's *Third Canto of Childe Harold, Manfred,* and *The Prisoner of Chillon.* Polidori, outclassed intellectually, became the butt of Byron's sadistic humor when he wrote poetry with phrases like "the goiter'd idiot of the Alps"; and Mary, at first, worked on some stories.

But before the summer was over the 18-year-old Mary and the 20-year-old Polidori began the two novels that have become classics of popular literature; her *Frankenstein* and his *The Vampyre.* By doing so they proved the point of Kenneth Burke's ironic epigram: "Most of us are such conformists that in the company of geniuses we would show talent, too." When the combined catalytic presence of Byron and Shelley ended, neither Polidori nor Mary Shelley ever wrote anything comparable to the novels begun during that extraordinary summer.

Daytimes the ambitious young intellectuals wrote seriously and read and discussed and laughed at the outside world of ordinary square-shaped people. But at night it was different. Subdued, they clung together by candlelight and fireplace at Byron's Villa

Diodati and relaxed by telling the most horrifying ghost stories they could remember.

At first it was great fun, but then a strange inevitability seized them and they could not stop telling ghost stories. They became a group of compulsive talkers and listeners whose Scheherazade lives seemed to depend upon their nightly story telling. The social gatherings became séances, and for weeks they descended deeper and deeper into the inferno of tormented dead who came back to haunt the guilty living—the fictional nightmares stirring up their private nightmares so that soon the nightly séances were transformed into a bizarre form of group therapy.

Byron unburdened himself of an anguished story (Mrs. Shelley later recalled) about "a young cousin named Thryza," who was always on his agonized conscience. She adored him and had borne him two children, but when he had refused to marry her she had committed suicide.

His constant torment, he declared, centered around his desire to erect a tombstone for Thryza, a desire that could not be fulfilled because, in obedience to the barbaric law then still in effect, she had been buried under a crossroads with a stake driven through her heart!

It was a chilling story that had its desired effect upon his highly impressionable companions; but, after 152 years of searching, Byron's biographers have not been able to find any trace of Thryza or her two children by Byron. She probably never existed, and some Byronists have insisted that actually Thryza was John Edleston, one of Byron's "humble" boy lovers. The great novelist Stendhal knew Byron very well and, after observing him closely for several months, became convinced that Byron sometimes confessed to "heinous crimes" that he had never committed and had in fact invented. Byron seemed to derive a peculiar Marquis de Sadisfaction from such confessions —from a perverse self-punishing desire to be regarded as a Satanic monster.

Then, on June 16, 1816, at Villa Diodati—the developing drama suddenly reached its high climax. It did so in a manner that leads one to conclude that the "Satanic" perverse Byron cunningly contrived the program for that evening to drive a wedge between Shelley and Mary so that he could sadistically observe their reactions (especially Mary's) as they squirmed guiltily under his nasty bisexually motivated attacks. Edward Trelawney, an intimate friend of both Shelley and Byron once said, "Byron was the real snake—a dangerous mischief-maker; his wit or humor might force a grim smile, or a hollow laughter, but savored more of pain than playfulness."

(Like his celebrated Don Juan, Lord Byron had a genius for inflicting savage emotional injuries upon those who adored him. Then, in William Blake's phrase, he "caught their shrieks in cups of gold," added his own exquisite remorse, and packaged the resulting sadomasochistic delicatessen as the superb poems that became runaway bestsellers in all of Europe.)

The evening of June 16 began with Byron reading a German ghost story about a man who kisses his bride on their wedding night and sees to his horror that she has become transformed into the dreadful moldering corpse of a woman whom he had deserted. The choice of that particular story, so evocative of the tragic, deserted Harriet in the Shelley-Harriet-Mary triangle—had to be Byronic mischief!

When his first surgical thrust seemed to have no

visibly bloody effect upon his victim, Byron (who makes any Edward Albee character look like a spayed pussycat) then attacked the Shelleys by reciting *Christabel*, the diabolical supernatural poem written by Samuel Taylor Coleridge, a close family friend of the Godwins. Byron, with inside family information given to him by the equally mischievous Claire, had deduced that *Christabel*, begun shortly after the death in childbirth of Mary Wollstonecraft in 1797 but then only recently published, was based upon the story of Mary Shelley and her mother.

Christabel is a young noblewoman whose mother had "died in the hour that [she] was born." In a dark forest at midnight Christabel encounters a damsel in distress named Geraldine. Christabel does not know that Geraldine is an evil incarnation of her dead mother and invites her to spend the rest of the night at her castle.

If the cold and reserved Mary recognized what Byron was up to, she gave no outward sign and stonily refused to perform in the cruel charade staged by Byron for his own delight and that of his Claire and Polly-Dolly.

But all of this was much too close to home for the highly vulnerable, hair-trigger Shelley. When Byron came to the scene in *Christabel* in which Geraldine disrobes before her daughter and thundered the line "Behold her bosom!" Shelley suddenly got the point of Byron's devious homophilic and antifeminist warning: Residing in the body of his Mary was an evil ghostly witch for whom he was the next victim. He sprang to his feet as if shot, grabbed a candle, and ran screaming through Villa Diodati! After a wild Keystone Kop chase he was finally captured and firmly held while Byron dashed cold water in his face and Dr. Polidori quieted him with ether. Later Shelley cagily explained that Geraldine had reminded him of the fabled witch of Sussex, who had two or three evil eyes in her breasts. Then he had glanced over at Mary's bosom, and it had stared back evilly at him. (Note to Percy Bysshe Shelley: Perhaps you should have gone out the front door of Villa Diodati and kept right on running, Mr. Shelley—Byron, Coleridge, and the fabled witch from your boyhood Sussex were trying to tell you something!)

It was then, a few minutes after Shelley's flight and splashdown, that Byron made his historic suggestion that each of them should try to write a ghost story; on the following morning they began. Byron began a story about a vampire but soon gave it up because he and Shelley were working on a much higher literary plateau; he very condescendingly—and foolishly—gave the story idea to Polidori. All summer long Polidori had been unable to conceal his jealousy of the profoundly intellectual Byron-Shelley friendship. Sometimes the two poets ran away from him as though he were an obnoxious kid sister, and once he even hysterically challenged Shelley to a pistol duel over a trifling matter. Polidori was cruelly dismissed by Byron at the end of summer and got his eternal revenge by making Byron the villain of his now celebrated *The Vampyre.*

Mario Praz has written, in *The Romantic Agony,* his phenomenal book about the great influence of the Marquis de Sade upon "Romantic" literature (in which he gives Byron an entire chapter), "Polidori elaborated Byron's vampire sketch by weaving suggestions into it from Lady Caroline Lamb's *Glenarvon* written in 1816." Lady Caroline, a "golden-haired sprite" and the most vindictive of Byron's discarded mistresses, put the lady-killing Byron into her novel as the perfidious Ruthven Glenarvon, who is finally carried off to hell by a Devil in drag—masquerading as one of Glenarvon-Byron's suicidal victims.

Byron may have been a terror in the boudoir, but he never publicly brawled with his victims, and he had pretended to ignore Lady Lamb's witty, way-below-the-belt attack. But he did manage to have the absolute last word in the unpleasant affair. Eight years later Byron's heartless body (his heart was buried at Missolonghi) was returned to England and sent to his home village of Hucknall-Torkard for burial. On July 12, 1824, according to George Brandes, a man and woman out for their morning ride passed the slow hearse. On a sudden impulse the woman stopped, rode back, and asked who was in the hearse. When she was told, "It's Lord Byron," Lady Caroline Lamb fainted and fell off her horse.

John Polidori went a spiteful step farther than Lady Caroline had and made Byron the vampire of his novel. When the book was published in 1819, the vampire was recognized at once by English readers as an accurate emotional portrait of his lordship.

And that, my dear little kiddies, is how Lord Byron, the romantic idol of Western culture, made himself the model for all the later blood-sucking vampires of horror literature, drama, and films, including Bela Lugosi's *Count Dracula*—and doomed himself to haunt the wasteland of late late shows for all eternity.

Shelley also began a novel, based on his boyhood flirtations with the dead, but soon tired of it and wisely decided to write his "Hymn to Intellectual Beauty" instead.

At first Mary could not think of an idea for the group's supernatural parlor competition, but just two evenings after Byron suggested the pastime (June 18), the idea of *Frankenstein* came to her as a result of an excited discussion between Byron and Shelley. Byron constantly read and recited passages from *Prometheus Bound* of Aeschylus; and Shelley was then laying the groundwork for his great *Prometheus Unbound*. There are several versions of the ancient myth, but to the young poets at Villa Diodati Prometheus was eternally punished for his two acts of divine civil disobedience. When Zeus became convinced that the quarrelsome human race he had created was unredeemable, and decided on total genocide by freezing, Prometheus saved us with the lightning-fire he stole from Heaven. He was also punished for infringing Zeus's monopoly when he created men of clay and gave them life.

Shelley and Byron speculated enthusiastically about the possibility of creating a new form of immortality to be controlled by Promethean doctors. "Perhaps," Mary recalled in the 1831 edition of her *Frankenstein*, "perhaps a corpse could be re-animated, galvanism had given token of such things. Perhaps the component parts of a creature could be manufactured . . . and endued with vital warmth." (This was, I believe, a stirring of her frantic desire to resurrect her dead mother, and echoed a touching journal entry of March 19, 1815, about the child who had died a few weeks after its birth: "Dreamed that my little baby came to life again; that it had only been cold and we rubbed it before the fire, and it lived. Awaken and find no baby.")

"That night," wrote Mary, "when I placed my head upon my pillow, I did not sleep. My imagination possessed and guided me, gifting the images that arose in my mind with a vividness far beyond the usual bond of reverie. I saw—with shut eyes, but acute mental vision—I saw the pale student of unhallowed arts besides the thing he had put together. I saw the hideous phantasm of a man stretched out and then, on the working of some powerful engine, show signs of life and stir with an uneasy half-vital motion.

"I have found it!" continued Mary, "what terrified me will terrify others; and I need only describe the spectre which haunted my midnight pillow. On the morrow I announced that I had thought of a story. At first I thought of a few pages only, but Shelley urged me to develop it to greater length; and but for his incitements it would never have taken the form in which it was presented to the world."

Dr. Victor Frankenstein's Monster was conceived on June 19, 1816, in the bed jointly occupied by Mary Wollstonecraft Godwin (later Shelley) and Percy Bysshe Shelley. After fourteen months of gestation (monsters take longer), he was born (completed) on September 1, 1817, and christened (published) in 1818—more than 150 years ago.

When the anonymously published *Frankenstein* first appeared, some book reviewers thought it was written by Percy Shelley, because they "recognized" his ideas; and Mary was still unknown as a writer. (I think *Frankenstein* was a collaboration.) The theatrical possibilities of the book were perceived at once, but, because of Shelley's reputation as an uncompromising atheist and critic of the establishment, no theatrical producer would touch it. But in 1823, about a year after Shelley drowned, the first dramatic production of *Frankenstein; or the Modern Prometheus* appeared under the totally compromised title, *Presumption: or The Fate of Frankenstein.* It was an immediate success and made Mary Shelley famous.

The novel that had been written as a sympathetic account of a failed experiment by a would-be savior of mankind was turned upside down. It became instead the first in an unending series of anti-intellectual science-fiction dramas, comedies, and even musical comedies about "mad scientists" who "try to play God" and "ferret out the hidden secrets of Mother Nature" in order to gain an evil control over the rest of us wholesome, God-fearing folk.

Since 1823, Mary Shelley's "waking nightmare" of June 18, 1816, has been happily shared by tens of millions of horror consumers—most of whom think that the Monster's name is Frankenstein. The confusion is the result of misleading titles like *The Bride of Frankenstein*, *Abbott and Costello Meet Frankenstein*, and *I Was a Teen-Aged Frankenstein*—and of the inverted characterization of Dr. Frankenstein as the villain and the Monster as *his* God-appointed punisher.

But Mary Shelley had something quite different in mind when she wrote her book. While she was under the magnetic influence of Shelley she agreed with him that scientists are among the noble benefactors of mankind. But soon after Shelley died in 1822 she became religious, perhaps because of her fear that she was next in line to be punished by God for her guilt-by-association with Shelley. She even piously invoked the Deity in the 1831 edition of *Frankenstein* and endorsed the public misinterpretation of her own novel—agreeing that Dr. Frankenstein is justly punished because he tampered with God's pre-ordained biological cycle of life and death.

Mary Shelley was able to abandon the Shelleyan

ideas about science because, as one discovers from reading her novel, she had more personal reasons for writing the book. Actually, behind the facade of Gothic horror and science fiction, Mary Shelley wrote an allegory of the disastrous consequences of love denied to children by parents concerned only with the fulfillment of their own desires. She was thinking of her own Dr. Frankenstein-like father's campaign to convert her into the supergirl who must replace her great mother.

This interpretation is not merely conjectural. Mary Shelley, a great one for unconsciously—yes—naïvely, revealing her innermost secrets, wrote a novel (*Mathilda,* 1819) shortly after the publication of *Frankenstein. Mathilda* is about a young woman whose "brilliant, beautiful and adored" mother dies in giving birth to her and whose vengeful father incestuously substitutes her for her mother! Mary actually gave this lulu to her father for publication and then complained later that "for reasons unknown" he had done absolutely nothing to have it published. It was never published in her lifetime.

Mary Shelley carefully explained in her preface to the 1831 edition of *Frankenstein* (she admitted that Shelley had written the preface to the first edition) that she had never intended her book to be a "mere horror tale" but a psychological study; and revealed that she had based it thematically on one of the stories told at Villa Diodati on the traumatic night of June 16, 1816. It was the story of a sinful founder of his race whose miserable doom it was to bestow the kiss of death upon all of the younger sons of his ill-fated house. When the boys reached the threshold of manhood, he would appear in black armour like the ghost of Hamlet's father and would kiss the forehead of the sleeping boys, who from that hour would wither on the stalk.

The films, including my own favorite *Bride of Frankenstein,* give us a morally corrupt, even deranged scientist, whose creature—through the mistake of a half-witted lab assistant—is given the brain of a murderer instead of the genius brain selected by the doctor.

But Mary Shelley's original Dr. Frankenstein failed, not for supernatural reasons but because he made two terrible human mistakes. The first was technical and forgivable. He aspired to build a superman, beautiful in mind and soul, with the finest bodies and organs and attributes he could obtain. But the extreme complexities of the task slowed him down, and his biological materials he used gradually deteriorated. When he finally succeeded in vitalizing his assembled man, he found that instead of a radiant superman, he had created an incredibly ugly creature—from which he fled in horror.

That reaction of horror—and here we have the innermost core of *Frankenstein*—that reaction to his own "brainchild" was Dr. Frankenstein's second and fatal mistake—"his kiss of death." The well-meaning scientist did not realize that though his re-born creature was *outwardly* hideous and therefore a failure, it was *inwardly* a sensitive human being with a potential for good or evil, for love or hatred. Like all advanced living organisms, Frankenstein's creature could not tolerate rejection—and ran away from his visibly disgusted and disappointed creator.

This is an extreme working out in fantasy of Mary Shelley's own situation: Early in life Mary knew—as every child in such a predicament knows infallibly

—that she could not successfully meet the Olympian challenge from her father and rightfully harbored a deep unconscious grievance against the man who had created her and then denied her love or forgiveness when she failed to replace his prestigious lost wife.

If Percy Bysshe Shelley was the model for the half of Dr. Victor Frankenstein who longed to bring the dead back to life, then William Godwin must be nominated as the model for the other half—the emotionally deficient Dr. Frankenstein—who turned away in disgusted disappointment from his own creation when it failed to live up to his expectations.

Mary Shelley very cleverly won sympathy and understanding for the Monster by assigning most of the key explanations of her melodrama to the Monster himself. We know the Monster from the various films as a creature who had not yet learned to use his vocal cords and who could utter only strangulated animal sounds. But in the novel the Monster, also called Devil, Wretch, Abhorred Entity, Detested Form, Odious Companion, Horror, Hideous Phantasm, and Vile Insect—speaks perfect French. Whenever he is not being hotly pursued by lynch mobs, who refuse to let him utter a single bon mot, Mary Shelley's Monster delivers superbly elegant monologues similar in style to the useless harangues shouted from the tumbril by Robespierre on his way to Madame Guillotine.

In one such monologue, lasting forty pages without a single interruption, the Hideous Phantasm explains how he managed to learn French so well. The reincarnated creature, after running away from his massive rejection by Dr. Frankenstein, wanders aimlessly through the high Alps and comes to a great forest in Germany, where he lives for more than a year on nuts and berries. In this parody of John Milton's *Paradise*

Lost (Shelley read it aloud to Mary while she was at work on *Frankenstein*) the great forest is a symbolic Garden of Eden.

In the forest the child-like, noble Creature (he does not become transformed into a Monster until he is persecuted for his ugliness) discovers an exiled French family, the De Laceys. The De Laceys, an idealized version of the Godwin family, are never aware of the Creature's presence, and he eavesdrops on them daily through a chink in the wall of their cottage. He learns French and becomes educated by overhearing them as they read from and discuss many profound books. The entirely malleable creature adopts all of their political and social opinions—mainly derived from the writings of William Godwin and Mary Wollstonecraft. He weeps for the poor and becomes outraged at the cruelty of kings and tyrants. He even becomes very distressed at the plight of the American Indians!

(At this point, two images linking the author with her "monster" comes irresistibly to mind: First is that of a little girl, the physical continuation or "resurrection" of Mary Wollstonecraft Godwin, seated on the periphery of a circle of great intellectuals in her father's home. She listens silently and unnoticed as they discuss and read aloud from their books. The second is of little Mary at the age of eight eavesdropping from behind a parlor sofa as the great Coleridge recites his immortal (and frightening) *Rime of the Ancient Mariner* based on Godwin's axiom that "the death of love freezes the heart and causes unbearable loneliness and destructiveness.")

The creature completes his voyeuristic Godwin-Shelley education by avidly reading three books that he finds lying on the ground like apples fallen from the Tree of Knowledge: Goethe's *Sorrows of Werther,* Plutarch's *Lives,* and Milton's *Paradise Lost.*

From his very close study of *Paradise Lost,* the creature deduces that he is an incarnation of the rejected characters in John Milton's great classic. From Dr. Frankenstein's first reactions to him and from some encounters with people in the forest, he has already come to realize that he is an object of horror to human beings; when he looks into the pools from which he drinks and compares himself with the De Laceys, he sees that he is monstrously ugly. The innocent creature becomes a monster and a killer when he realizes that he is a misfit Adam permanently denied entrance to human society and at once identifies himself with the defeated sympathetic Satan of *Paradise Lost.* God, he concludes sadly, has a very quarrelsome attitude toward his creatures and is merciless toward their weaknesses and failings.

By arriving at these conclusions, the creature (a veritable Edmund Wilson among monsters!) joined the company of advanced critics of John Milton: Percy Bysshe Shelley, William Blake, and much later, T. S. Eliot and William Empson. Blake wrote that "John Milton was of the Devil's party without knowing it," for liking Satan as much as he did. Shelley agreed with Blake: "Milton alleged no virtue of his God over his Satan." And the late Mr. Eliot hinted broadly that John Milton's Old Testament Jehovah was too Jewish for him, definitely not the sort of God with whom he planned to spend his Anglican eternity.

The views of the Monster belong of course to Shelley, who expressed similar views in this *Prometheus Unbound,* in which he attacked Milton's Christian God under the code-name of Zeus. My favorite opinion from this once-fashionable arena of literary-theological disputation comes from William Empson's book *Milton's God.* Professor Empson believes that John Milton was actually very fond of God and wrote *Paradise Regained* in order to give Him another chance to prove His humanity!

Theatrical and film producers have never presented the original conception of the monster because they have either preferred to follow already-established theatrical misconceptions slavishly or believed that audiences cannot accept the story of a creature who has educated himself from scratch in a few months by eavesdropping on conversations and reading only three books.

But the creature-turned-monster did not start from scratch. His peeping-Tom, Adam-and-Eve self-education was only the refresher course for a composite being who was "made up" of people who had lived before him. His body was that of a man, but my accumulated observations tell me that his spirit, his intellect, and the highest priority for resurrection among the several persons within him primarily and definitely belong to Mary Wollstonecraft.

The poor woman was never allowed to rest! First, Godwin paraded her before her little daughter as a totally unfair rival. Coleridge exhumed her to play the unflattering role of the evil witch Geraldine in his poem *Christabel.* Shelley fell in love with her image, superimposed as it was on the alluring body of Mary, in the Old St. Pancras graveyard. Beastly Byron borrowed her from Coleridge for use in the Villa Diodati charade that scared the wits out of Shelley and sent him off yodeling in terror at what she might do to him. And now her daughter Mary had written an entire book in which she revived her, monsterized her, killed her, and with that act of exorcism hoped that the spirit of Mary Wollstonecraft would remain undisturbed forever afterward.

Do you need a little more convincing? When Dr. Frankenstein finally succeeds in giving life to his creature and becomes horrified by its terrible ugliness, he races out of his laboratory to his bedroom. Finally, exhausted, he falls asleep and dreams that he sees his fiancée:

> Delighted and surprised, I embraced her, but as I imprinted the first kiss on her lips, they became livid with the hue of death . . . and *I beheld the corpse of my dead mother in my arms* . . . a shroud enveloped her form and graveworms crawling in the flannel. *I started up from my sleep in horror and I beheld the wretch—the miserable monster I had created.* I escaped and rushed downstairs. [my italics]

In this single short scene we see that all of the traumatic events of June 16, 1816, are repeated: The "kiss of death" story told by Byron merges with the image of a long-dead mother returned from the grave who then, upon the wakening of Frankenstein is transformed into the image of the newly created Monster. It also contains the image of Shelley's mad flight through Villa Diodati when Byron stabbed him with the realization that he was threatened by the ghost of Mary Wollstonecraft now residing in the body of his wife.

The novel *Frankenstein* reaches its finale in a very exotic setting. Dr. Frankenstein becomes convinced that he must destroy his creature and pursues him all the way to the Arctic Circle, to a desolate area somewhere north of Archangel, Russia. He cannot catch the superhumanly powerful Phantasm and finally, exhausted in body and mind, takes refuge in a ship and dies—but not before telling his tragic story to Captain Walton, an English explorer. At the very end of the book the Monster also comes to the ship and, over the open coffin of Dr. Frankenstein, explains to Walton (the book's narrator) his reasons for killing so many innocent people and for his intense self-loathing. He does so in terms that would be instantly endorsed by many mouth-to-mouth psychiatrists.

The monster pleads that Dr. Frankenstein, whom he calls his "father-creator," brought him back from the dead but then denied him his love or the possibility of love from anyone else. By creating him eight feet tall and so very ugly, Frankenstein had made him the victim of normal humans, who either fainted dead away at the mere sight of him or tried to exterminate him as if he were an animal. Consumed with loneliness he had begged the doctor to construct a female companion for him. Finally, under threats of death to his family, Dr. Frankenstein did begin to construct a bride for him, but destroyed it when he realized "that a race of devils would be propagated upon the earth who might make the very existence of the species of man a condition precarious and full of terror." The creature sums up the Miltonian meaning of *Frankenstein:*

> When I run over the frightful catalogue of my sins, I cannot believe that I am the same creature whose thoughts were once filled with sublime and transcendent visions of the beauty and majesty of goodness. And it is even so: the fallen angel becomes a malignant devil. Yet even that enemy of God and man had friends and associates in his desolation: I am alone.

And so, raging, the oedipal Monster declares it is

his "father-creator's" terrible rejections of him that are responsible for all the murders that have occurred. He would now destroy the last surviving actor in the tragedy, himself.

After stating his case with remarkable insight for a self-educated pre-Freudian Monster, the poor nameless son-of-a-botch leaps out a cabin window onto an ice floe and drifts off after exclaiming:

> I shall ascend my funeral pile triumphantly, and exult in the agony of the torturing flames. The light of that conflagration will fade away; my ashes will be swept away into the sea. My spirit will sleep in peace; or if it thinks, it will surely not think thus. Farewell.

So ends the monster.

With great insight and compassion, Mary Shelley gave Dr. Frankenstein his alibi too. He reveals, in a letter to a friend, the precise emotional trauma that led him to create the abortive Creature-turned-Monster. When he was 14 years old, he wrote, he found a book in his father's library written by the occult German philosopher M. Cornelius Agrippa (one of Shelley's boyhood heroes). Naïvely, he had tried to communicate his excitement about Agrippa's ideas to his father. "But," wrote Frankenstein, "my father hurt me badly by casually dismissing Agrippa's ideas as 'sad trash.' If, instead of this offhand dismissal, he had taken the pains to explain to me that the principles of Agrippa had been exploded by modern science, I should have thrown Agrippa aside, and have contented my imagination, warmed as it was, by returning with greater ardour to my former studies. It is even possible that the train of ideas would never have received the fatal impulse that led to my ruin."

Mary Shelley apparently succeeded in exorcising her mother's restless spirit and her own monstrous sense of guilt by writing *Frankenstein* (that's why she never wrote its sequel!), but she soon became permanently involved with two other ghosts. After her husband's death the beautiful and famous Mary Shelley, only 25, never remarried. She settled down with her surviving son, Percy Florence (the other three children died in infancy), and saw Percy Florence outlast Harriet's son, Charles, and inherit the Shelley title and great fortune. Several very eligible men, including the celebrated composer John Howard Payne, fell in love with her and proposed marriage.

But Mary, who late in life wrote in her journal, "Poor Harriet, to whose fate I owe so many of my own heavy sorrows, as the atonement claimed by fate for her death," preferred to spend the rest of her life living in her memory-haunted house as "the spiritual concubine" of the watery ghosts of Percy Bysshe and Harriet Shelley. She turned down John Howard Payne and his ever-so-humble "Home, Sweet Home."

William James Sidis

THE STREETCAR NAMED PARADISE LOST

Conductor, when you receive a fare,
Punch in the presence of the passenjare!
A blue trip slip for an eight-cent fare,
A buff trip slip for a six-cent fare,
A pink trip slip for a three-cent fare,
Punch in the presence of the passenjare!

CHORUS

Punch, brothers, punch with care!
Punch in the presence of the passenjare!

—MARK TWAIN'S OBSESSIVE JINGLE (1876)

I HAVE MET some very interesting collectors of trivia, but the most interesting of all I can never meet. He was before my time. He was the legendary William James Sidis, who attracted a great deal of attention during the 1930s, when *The New Yorker* ran a short article about him. The late Mr. Sidis was the son of Boris Sidis, a Russian-born professor of abnormal psychology at Harvard University, who specialized in the study of multiple or split personalities.

If we are to believe the legend that surrounds both father and son, Professor Sidis was convinced that geniuses are not born—and that he could create them with his scientific teaching methods. When his son was less than six months old (in 1898), he began to teach him to read by hanging alphabet blocks over the baby's crib. At the age of two the infant Sidis was banging away meaningfully at a typewriter, and by the time that he was six he knew a great deal of Latin and Greek and had even invented a perpetual calendar in the form of a computer disk.

Professor Sidis' teaching methods seemed to be working extremely well, and William James Sidis was presented to Harvard University for matriculation at the age of 9. But the university administration decided that he was emotionally immature and told him to come back when he was 11. (Sidis still holds the distinction of having been the youngest student ever to attend Harvard, beating out little Cotton Mather, who entered Harvard in 1674 at the age of 12.)

In his first year (1909), the prodigious child created a sensation with a lecture to the science faculty on the mathematics of fourth-dimensional bodies. A brilliant future was predicted for him. But something happened soon after he began his studies at Harvard. He had a nervous breakdown at twelve and was transferred for a time to his father's sanatorium at Portsmouth, New Hampshire. Later he returned to school and was graduated magna cum laude.

Buckminster Fuller remembers Sidis at Harvard. He told me: "Most students considered him a freak. He was 16 when I knew him, but his parents still sent him to school dressed like a boy of 12. In those days a boy automatically put on long trousers when he was 14, but Willy Sidis still wore Little Lord Fauntleroy short pants and high-buttoned shoes. Some of us thought he was being dangerously overloaded, and he showed some signs of distress, but no one imagined anything but the greatest success for him."

Shortly after he was graduated, young Sidis joined the Socialist youth movement and took part in some demonstrations. During one May Day "riot" he was arrested for allegedly having assaulted a police officer on a streetcar, but he was never prosecuted or jailed.

Then, abruptly, he withdrew from all formal academic and intellectual life and became a complete "loner." He took the lowliest of jobs and always refused promotion; he quit job after job when people learned of his unfulfilled genius; and then, except for a few minor interests, like the culture of the lost tribe of Okammakammassett Indians and the lost continent of Atlantis, he devoted the rest of his life to peridromophily: riding in streetcars and the collection of streetcar transfers.

William James Sidis amassed an enormous number of streetcar transfers and even published a book, *Notes on the Collection of Transfers,* at his own expense before he died in 1944. So goes the legend.

Why did the remarkable young man give up a life of advanced scholarship, a life that promised great intellectual rewards for himself and society? Was he simply a human computer who had burned out his irreplaceable basic fuses? Or did he come to the conclusion that the values of the life for which he was being molded were false; and that he would dramatize his rebellion against his father and the intellectual establishment by devoting his intelligence to the collection of trifles?

Perhaps there is a clue in the irony that Boris Sidis named his son after "his revered master," the American philosopher William James, who had written:

> I am against bigness and greatness in all their forms, and *with* the invisible molecular moral forces that work from individual to individual, stealing through the crannies of the world like so many soft rootlets, or like the capillary oozing of water, and yet rending the hardest monuments of man's pride, if you give them time. The bigger the unit you deal with, the

hollower, the more brutal, the more mendacious is the life displayed.

So I am against all big successes and big results, and in favor of the eternal forces of truth that always work in the individual and immediately unsuccessful way, underdogs always, until history comes, long after they are dead, and puts them on top.

Intrigued by all the ideas clustering around these possibilities, I began to take a hard look at the journalistic myths surrounding William James Sidis. Most of them seemed to oversimplify, to draw conclusions from scanty evidence, and to pass quick judgments on a very rare genius caught in a unique situation.

In one Sunday-supplement article, written in a tremulous style in the early 1940s, Sidis was compared "with two other infant prodigies who have vanished from the scene after reaching the pinnacle of fame." One of the vanished was little Miss Shirley Temple, and the other was Master Baby Leroy.

The comparison with Shirley Temple is now more than a bit wobbly, because, as everyone knows, Shirley simply outgrew her enchanting five-year-old personality and is a normal wife, mother, Republican, and delegate to the United Nations. But the comparison between the infant prodigy Leroy and the infant prodigy Sidis was not all that far fetched. Baby Leroy achieved immortality in the film *The Old Fashioned Way* when the great W. C. Fields jealously booted him in his little behind for stealing too many scenes. Sidis was also a victim of a similar boot in the behind, metaphorically speaking.

(Another boy prodigy, Frank Harris, never forgot a similar indignity, and at the age of seventy, bitterly described an incident from his English grammar school days. His teacher had told his class that the essayist Lord Macauley was a genius with a phenomenal memory. "Lord Macauley," he rhapsodized, "once declared that if through some highly selective disaster every copy of John Milton's *Paradise Lost* should vanish from the face of the earth, *he* could remedy the loss because he had memorized it as a boy, and could still recite it perfectly."

Frank Harris, aged 12, immediately signaled for attention and asked: "Sir, is that a hard thing to do?" The teacher, stressing the word *Lord* answered, "*Lord* Macauley was a genius. When you have learned just a fraction of that great classic, you will understand how difficult it is."

Young Harris, who had a very fine memory, saw the chance to impress his teacher and classmates, and immediately began to memorize the long classic. A few weeks later he announced to his teacher, "Please, sir, I know all of *Paradise Lost* by heart. Would you like to hear me recite it?" The teacher glared at him and snarled, "Sit down, Harris!" After class, Harris wrote, he was beaten and kicked by his classmates for such a vulgar display of genius. (By his act of memorizing *Paradise Lost,* the plebian Harris set into motion the wheels of a strange black comedy: he made of himself an innocent travesty of Milton's great drama, for he had become a juvenile Satan who had fallen from grace for having dared to compete with the mental power of the Lord—Lord Macauley that is.)

Several writers who tackled the Sidis story after his death in 1944 hinted darkly of heavenly punishment visited on Professor Sidis for his exhibition of hubris —or was it plain old *chutzpah?* He was compared to Svengali and to Dr. Frankenstein. It is a very far cry from the fantasized Gothic horrors of *Frankenstein* to the mundane story of the scholarly Professor Sidis and his little supermannequin, but some aspects of the old romance were foisted on them anyway.

"God was angry with the upstart Harvard don for presuming to improve on His handiwork and had punished the father in the Old Testament way—through his son. The Lord rolled back the I.Q. of young Sidis to its preintervention level, turned him against his own father, and made him obsessively addicted to the collection of transfer trivia."

Later, as I explored the story of the Sidises, I found this kind of speculation infectious, and I actually began to believe that there was a touch of relevance to such fantasies. I continued my investigation of the young genius, hoping to find something in his bizarre story that might throw some new light on the deeper motivations of trivia collecting, including my own. (Confession: I have never been able to collect streetcar transfers because of Sidis. Illogically, I own many fine railroad and streetcar tickets, but I draw the line at transfers. The ghost of Sidis warns me that my interest in trivia might go over the line into a mania for hoarding worthless junk. This is not likely but lends a little comedy-drama to my collecting, to imagine such a dread possibility, and it is pleasant to have a personal ghost in attendance. It lends class to the apartment.)

After an article of mine, in which I mentioned Sidis, appeared in a magazine in 1967, I received a letter from Edward T. ("Ted") Frankel, an auditor who had worked with Sidis during the late 1920s and who offered to show me his collection of Sidis material. Frankel has a passion for mathematics and collects material about "crank" mathematicians—that happy breed of eccentrics who, in defiance of the holy canons of mathematics, persist in trying to square the circle, trisect the angle, and discover the precise algebraic equation that will prove the existence of God.

Ted Frankel told me that he had always been intrigued by Sidis, perhaps because Sidis was a mathematical genius manqué, and it was moving to see that he still retained his original feeling of distress and sympathy for the tragic young misfit whom he had known nearly forty years ago.

In 1928 the National Industrial Conference Board, a research organization, hired Sidis to operate a Burroughs calculating machine for $25 a week. At first, he managed to keep his story secret, but when it was discovered that he knew higher mathematics he was immediately offered some advanced work with the promise of more money. But Sidis, who had been through the same situation before, stubbornly refused and stayed with his calculator.

"He was good with that machine," said Frankel. "So remarkably good, in fact, that his immediate supervisor, J. M. Robertson, became obsessed with the idea that Sidis was really performing all his calculations mentally and only pretending to operate the machine to throw him off the track! A hilarious Charlie Chaplin comedy developed, with Robertson watching Sidis like a hawk but pretending not to, and Sidis pretending not to know that Robertson was watching him. But it was no match. Sidis ran that machine right under Robertson's nose so cleverly that Robertson never knew what in hell was going on."

While Sidis was employed at the NICB, according to Frankel, several experts in the organization tried to involve him in discussions of mathematics or philosophy, but he insisted angrily that he had forgotten everything that he had known. "But on one occasion he slipped," said Frankel. "Somebody showed him a new set of tables that had been prepared by some of our top experts as an aid in solving certain complicated statistical problems. The tables were useful but admittedly incomplete. Sidis studied them for a while and suggested a simple way of eliminating all the difficulties. It was obvious that he had forgotten *nothing*. After that brilliant demonstration, the pressure on Sidis to conform increased, he began to look and behave like a trapped animal, and finally he resigned.

"I really felt terribly sorry for him. He was like a child. He told me that he didn't know how to apply for another job and that it was useless to write letters of application because they were all thrown in wastebaskets. He really needed help. I spent many of my lunch hours going around to the offices of the big companies around Grand Central station trying to find a job for him. I told the office managers that Sidis was a wizard, but, since I knew that they would discover his story (people always did), I had to tell them that he was only interested in a subsistence job and that he would refuse any promotions. When they heard that, they said that they were definitely not interested. They didn't want to have a man like that around. Sidis left New York. Once or twice we got a postcard from him. Then he just disappeared."

When Ted Frankel left the room to fetch his Sidis material, I thought about the wayward young clerk whom he had tried to help during the 1920s. Sidis reminded me of the strikingly similar character in the deeply moving story—or is it a parable?—by Herman Melville, "Bartleby the Scrivener" (1853). It is compassionately narrated by a Wall Street lawyer who hired a strange young eccentric named Bartleby to copy law briefs at 4 cents a sheet. Bartleby was quite alone in the world and seemed to live only for his menial copying work, which he did very well.

But from the start, when he was asked to proofread copy as the other clerks did, or when he was offered more interesting work, Bartleby refused, murmured politely, "I prefer not to."

Then one morning he refuses his daily stint of work with the same polite words, "I prefer not to." After that, he does no work at all and sits all day staring out the window at a blank brick wall.

After some days, his unnerved employer offered Bartleby a substantial sum of money if he would simply leave. But the now entirely silent young man just shook his head. Finally, unable to cope with the situation, the employer vacated the premises, leaving the listless and uncomplaining Bartleby standing in the middle of an empty office!

At the story's end, the conscience-stricken employer tells us that, having been informed that Bartleby was in the city prison-poorhouse, he rushed there to help him. But he arrived too late. Bartleby had said "no" to life itself.

Many Melville scholars see in "Bartleby the Scrivener" a thinly veiled self-portrait, of its author, for shortly after he finished the story Melville withdrew from all formal intellectual life, quit writing professionally, and took a menial job as a customs inspector, a job that he held for most of the rest of his life. It seems that our greatest American novelist is also our greatest dropout.

The trolley train of thought that had carried me on an excursion back into time from Sidis to "Bartleby the Scrivener," with a detour to view the noble wreck of Herman Melville, now brought me back to Sidis. And just in time too, because Ted Frankel had returned with his copy of *Notes on the Collection of Transfers*, published by Sidis under the highly inelegant pseudonym of Frank Folupa, and some copies of the crudely hectographed bulletin written and published by Sidis, *The Peridromophile.*

I began to read the Sidis material with great expectations, but the book repelled me instantly. It is almost impenetrable. There are some surprising revelations in the writings of Sidis, to which we shall come soon, but their extraction required some very hard literary detective work. On reflection, I know that Sidis wanted it that way and craftily hid his bitter feelings among some of the most remarkable *idiot savant* material deliberately assembled.

Unlike other collectors of printed ephemera, Sidis showed no interest at all in transfers as specimens of the art of printing. He did make a slight token bow to "the educational values of transfers," mentioning that one item in his collection always reminded him of a ride that he had taken past the home of Paul Revere. And, surprisingly, I could find no trace at first of the legend of the forlorn little boy who found his only happiness riding the trolleys home from the emotional tortures inflicted upon him in the groves of Academe.

Instead the curious young man from Boston chose to write an unreadable treatise on the most minute details of the technical design of transfer forms. The transfers served as a guide to the operation and routing of streetcars through the labyrinth of large American cities at different times of the day, including rush hours.

The book is written from the point of view of the board of directors of a large municipal transportation system. In this corporate image Sidis seems to be chief traffic manager and efficiency engineer specializing in transfer systems. He plays the game to the hilt and dutifully prints patents issued to inventors of transfers. Here is one, issued to Mr. John Moran on October 26, 1924, which Sidis offers to the reader without comment on its value or application:

> A transfer ticket consisting of two portions, one of which is provided with indicia designating car route, or routes, on which the transfer is acceptable, and the date of issue; and the other of which comprises a series of adjoining, but divisible coupons each bearing a different unitary time limit, each of which is applicable to all parts of the said indicia.

At first I was impressed by the extraordinary intellectual game that Sidis had invented for himself, and I marveled at his mastery of the intricacies of its technology. But, after grappling with some of the material in the book, I experienced a growing uneasiness, a sensation that the whole thing was a put-on, a hoax of the first magnitude.

For example, one entire chapter consists of long lists of all the numbers on all the streetcar lines in Los Angeles, Hartford, Buffalo, Philadelphia, and New York City (all five boroughs). Sidis admitted that the listing was incomplete and regretted that space limitations made it impossible to list similar data for all the rest of the large cities in the United States! He also apologized for the listings because they were "made two years before the publication of the book and are now probably obsolete." Furthermore, his tone conveys that it hardly matters anyway, for no one else in the world could possibly be interested in such highly arcane material.

But perhaps the most extraordinary pages in *Notes on the Collection of Transfers* are those in which

Sidis tells of a journey during which he acquired forty transfers in one continuous chain of rides on the streetcars of New York City. As we are dealing with a man in the grip of an overriding mania, I have decided to include his log of that voyage of more than fifteen hours on a single day. It had to be done in one day because the transfers expired after a few hours. Nothing I found in the book reveals the compulsions of the man more clearly than does the following:*

> 14. Reversibility as Aid in Collection. The principle of reversibility of fares and transfers, as discussed above, is one of the greatest aids to a would-be collector in getting different varieties of transfer forms on any one system, and, where there are inter-company transfers, sometimes on several systems at once. This being such an important aid in indicating where a collector should look for new transfer forms, we may go into detail on this matter. The collector, let us say, arrives in New York City and takes a ride in a "green car" down Broadway. He may know from the guides or otherwise that "green cars" also run on 14th Street, and takes a chance asking for a transfer to West 14th Street. He gets a two-cent transfer marked as issued from "Broadway–7th Avenue Line South," and the right-hand coupon lists the transfer as good on 8th Street, 23rd Street or 34th Street east or west, or on Spring and Delancey east. By in turn boarding cars east and west at 14th Street and at 23rd Street bound for Broadway, and asking for a transfer north on Broadway (the reverse of the original ride), we get four more transfer forms; on Spring and Delancey west, still another form is obtained which, on examination, turns out to be issued

* Note to the reader: Obviously no one is expected to be *meshuga* enough to read this excerpt in its entirety. But it is included as an example of what a real 100% *meshuganer* can produce.

from that line in either direction. Similarly if we start out from a 34th Street car. Thus we get a total of seven transfer forms from that system. We can get two more from the 8th Street line by the same process, and, if we get on a westbound 8th Street car coming from East 10th Street, we will get another, thus bringing up the total number of forms to ten. We may further note that the 14th Street forms give transfer to 6th Avenue, 7th Avenue, or Lexington Avenue north or south and to Broadway south as well as north. The reverse of these give us seven more transfer forms; so that, after obtaining these, we have a total of seventeen. But this is not all. The Lexington Avenue forms indicate a transfer to 116th Street, and if we ask for a transfer to Lexington Avenue from a 116th Street car, we get, not a two-cent transfer, but a free transfer. Concluding that the reverse is also a free transfer, we try again to get transfers to 116th Street from Lexington Avenue cars bound north and south, and thus get two more free transfer forms. We now have twenty "green car" transfer forms, all obtained from the original one form by this reversibility principle. But again we may note that the repeat privilege on these two-cent transfers calls for a transfer from 116th Street to the Columbus-Lenox line: this turns out to be a two-cent transfer, good on the Columbus-Lenox line north or south. Trying this line both north and south and asking for transfer to 116th Street, we get two more two-cent transfer forms, thus bringing our total up to twenty-three, including twenty two-cent forms, or all the two-cent forms issued by that company. If a northbound Columbus Avenue car is taken at the most convenient point, the beginning of the line, we notice that many passengers pay fare in transfers, which could be either from the red cars on Broadway, or from the green Ninth Avenue cars. Presuming the latter, we try that and get a transfer form of the Ninth Avenue Company. One of the punch spaces reads "6th Ave. R.R." and taking the Sixth Avenue cars both north and south, we get two more free transfer forms. Also the fact that a northbound

Ninth Avenue car transfers to a northbound Columbus Avenue car means that, by reversibility, a southbound Columbus Avenue car will give free transfer to the southbound Ninth Avenue cars, resulting in still another free transfer. So we have now obtained twenty-seven forms. But we may notice that the eastbound 23rd Street transfer form has the notation on the center coupon: "To 2nd Ave. Line N. at 34th St. from E. 34th St. Ferry Branch cars only with coupons attached." To get the return transfer, we get on a southbound car on Second Avenue and get a transfer to 23rd Street west: there being two car lines on Second Avenue, we get two transfer forms, this time from another system, and free transfers, not two-cent ones. Noting that these give transfer privilege to the 86th Street cars of the Second Avenue Railroad, we can get still another form as the reverse of that privilege. We now have thirty transfer forms, all distinct. But we may notice that our Second Avenue forms were free but that the reverse transfers were not free. So, taking a 23rd Street eastbound car again bound for the East 34th Street Ferry, we get this time a free transfer to Second Avenue, noting that it also covers a transfer to Fourth Avenue south, with a privilege of retransfer to 14th Street east. So we may look for transfer from Fourth Avenue south to 14th Street east, and, conversely, from 14th Street west to Fourth Avenue north, and again from there to 23rd Street west. We can get these provided we get on the car at or after the proper transfer point indicated by the retransfer. But these transfers indicate retransfer privileges through 23rd Street west to Broadway north, and again to 34th Street west. So we can look for transfers from 23rd Street west to Broadway north, and again from there to 34th Street west, and, by reversing, from 34th Street east to Broadway south, and from there to 23rd Street east. Such forms can be obtained, again provided we do not get on the car before the previous transfer junction of the series. Then, noting that the Fourth Avenue transfer forms give transfer to 34th Street east and to 86th Street, we can get a reverse form for

> both. In this way, starting with one sample transfer form on which the collector took a chance, the far reversibility principle finally leads us to obtain no less than forty distinct transfer forms on two different systems (or four systems, if we count the Ninth Avenue Railroad and the New York and Harlem traction lines as separate systems).

Sidis adds, "On the Public Service Railroad in New Jersey, a collector getting a single one-cent transfer anywhere in the system (collecting before October 1, 1923) could by the same plan, collect no fewer than one hundred and ten distinct transfer forms between New York and Philadelphia." Such a collecting voyage would have taken a minimum of *fifty hours of continuous traveling!*

Discouraged by a mania that seemed to be far greater than my talent for measuring it, understanding it, or even reading it, I was about to give up on the son of a gun, when I saw that in his preface he urged the "ordinary reader" ("That's me," I groaned) to skip all the technical stuff and read the last chapter. There I found some material that seemed promising and that eventually led me to the solution of the enigma.

The first glimmer of light came in the form of some rather daft "mnemonic poems" written by Sidis to help him memorize his beloved technical data and to commemorate certain important events in the history of streetcars.

His first verse was an epic poem, a saga of the ancient Indian bean hole which later became the Boston subway:

When the tribes of old foregathered at Shawmut's triple
hill

A great pit was dug in the hillside which all the tribes with beans would fill
When the council fires were lighted, and the Red Men of the East,
Could complete their council pow-pow by rejoicing in the feast.
Many years passed since these councils, and the pits were covered o'er
And the whites a mighty city built upon the Shawmut shore,
But the pit, revived, extended, was put to uses new,
As the world's first subway system from that ancient bean-hole grew.

He followed this poem with, first, a reprint of a poem that he had written at the age of fourteen to commemorate the opening of the Cambridge, Massachusetts, subway on March 23, 1912; second, "a verse to explain the company number of the routes as tried out on some of the lines in and around Boston in 1913;" and, third, a quatrain telling the reader how to find his way around Boston on the subway.

Sidis concluded his little anthology with

A Mother Goose alphabet to explain the letters on Los Angeles streetcars:

A is for *Adams,* well known man of state.
B is for *Brooklyn,* the borough so great.
C is for *Crown Hill,* or *Crooked Hill,* maybe.
D is for *Depot,* where stops the *Esspee* (Southern Pacific R.R.)
E is for *Eagle Rock,* towards the north,
F is on top of a car and stands for *Fourth.*

As I read these daffy mnemonic poems, I wondered why he had gone to the expense of publishing a book for himself alone. Was there anything hidden away in the mnemonics of the book, anything at all?

The last chapter of *Notes on the Collection of Transfers* was not easy to read, but the bloodhound in me persisted. Then I found something that made me sit up and really take notice: The book had just delivered its first important clue in the form of a "joke": "After a 'collegiate' subway riot, one of the 'rah-rah' boys arrested for assaulting an officer, said: 'But it's all a mistake! I didn't mean to strike a policeman. I thought he was a streetcar conductor!' " With this typical joke, expressed in the form of the slap-happy old-line burlesque theater ("Who was that *lady* I seen you with last night?" "That was *no* lady. That was my wife!"), William James Sidis began to reveal his secrets.

He was obviously referring to an actual incident in his life, but he has chosen to tell it in an abbreviated form. Spelled out, his message reads: "Ten years ago I became involved in a May Day demonstration in Boston, and I was arrested for assaulting an officer. But it was all a mistake. Something bad had happened to me while I was riding on a streetcar as a small boy, and I became so confused that I couldn't distinguish one figure of authority from another. I really wanted to attack a certain streetcar conductor, but in my confusion I attacked a police officer instead. (That was no policeman! That was my conductor!) Who was that certain streetcar conductor I wanted to attack? Read some more of my jokes, and maybe you will find out. But, remember, I am confessing all this in the form of jokes and nothing can be held against me."

A quick check of the humorous material published by William James Sidis in his book and in that section of his monthly *The Peridromophile* that he called "Rail-ery" showed that every joke, pithy expression, wisecrack, or anecdote contained an unmistakable reference to his disastrous childhood and adolescence. Concealed in his joke column was his message to the world. He was apprehensive about giving up his painful secrets. In order to protect himself, he presented them lightly disguised as little surrealistic skits.

But I remained wary of Sidis. Ted Frankel's story of the calculator duel between Sidis and Robertson came to mind. I also remembered that in 1937 Sidis had sued *The New Yorker* for invading his privacy. He claimed that, by reminding the public of his past as a prodigy, the magazine had made it very difficult for him to make a living. He protested that he had become an ordinary man and was willing to undergo intelligence tests to prove it; anyone calling him a genius was really trying to persecute him. Only a genius could have come up with such an argument! But the lawsuit was tossed out of court on the ground that the public's need to learn about him was greater than his need for privacy.

What a treat it would have been to witness this upside-down Oscar Wilde in a battle of wits with a sharp lawyer, the latter trying to prove that Sidis was a genius and Sidis using his genius to feign stupidity. It would have been the calculator duel all over again, and I would have bet my money on Sidis' genius to prove that he had none.

It was a role that he had played most of his life with great skill. Was it merely coincidence that four of his father's six books had dealt entirely with split or multiple personalities? It is my layman's guess that Sidis devoted a large part of his genius to inventing for himself and playing a role that would defy and evade all of the neat pre-Freudian classifications in his father's books.

It is easy to understand, then, why I asked myself: "What is this man *really* up to? What did he really have in mind when he published this transfer book, this sly, cryptic Baedeker to his inner feelings? Did this sardonic misanthrope suddenly hunger for understanding and approval? Or was he like Hamlet in the mad scenes, merely feigning the role of *Idiot savant,* acting the buffoon in some shrewdly stupid charades and talking foolishly in order to conceal his intention to kill the King?"

The witty moral of Edgar Allan Poe's "The Purloined Letter" is known to almost everyone: If you wish to hide something really important from experts in the art of searching, put it where they can't possibly miss it. With that purloined thought firmly in mind, I opened *Notes on the Collection of Transfers* to its title page and stared fearlessly at the uncouth pseudonym boldly exhibited there by Sidis.

Frank Folupa. What a name! Ted Frankel suggested that Folupa is an exact anagram for "foul pa," and that interpretation seems to fit from one point of view, but the name also suggests other variations, all distasteful and derogatory. There is: "fouled up," "frankly a flop," and inevitably the name of the lovable comic-strip character Joe Palooka, the powerful dunce who always manages to outwit his more intelligent enemies.

But, though the name of Frank Folupa does have such belittling connotations, I suspected that "lupa" meant something else. I looked it up in the Latin and Italian lexicons and found that Sidis had nothing at all comic in mind when he called himself Folupa.

The entire word cannot be translated, but its components can. A *fol* is a fib, a fable, a humbug, an old wives' tale, or nonsense. Its diminutive *foletta* means "imp" or "little devil." A *folle* is a frenzied, deranged, maniacal, insane, or mad person. And a *lupa*? A *lupa* is not only a she wolf but also a lewd woman, a prostitute, or a person having an inordinately greedy or wolfish appetite.

Suddenly the name Frank Folupa began to look like a very nasty graffito written on a fence by William James Sidis.

We must assume that Sidis, an accomplished Latinist from the age of six, knew the meanings, implications, and genders of the self-annihilating pseudonym that he invented to grace his cryptic book about transfers. Perhaps he reasoned that only a tiny handful of unsophisticated transfer collectors would ever see the book and that they would not bother to decode the pseudonym. The book was privately printed in a very small edition, and most of the copies were destroyed in a fire. But unfortunately the odious pseudonym has survived and we can only stand by, acutely embarrassed, and pretend not to notice the spectacle of a man who says, in effect: "I am a maniacal she wolf, a lewd prostitute, a humbug who performs nonsensical acts and then publishes the results in the form of a fable about streetcar transfers." Obviously Sidis knew that people regarded him as a wolf and went them several better.

I prefer to take the name of Folupa in its most charitable sense and to believe that our antihero admitted to being a maniacal wolfman who had published a fable or allegory in the form of a book about streetcar transfers.

For some readers, the motorman's bell of literary recall is now ringing: DING! DING! It is ringing loud and clear, for enough has been said about Sidis to enable them to spot the powerful resemblance between him and Harry Haller, the central character of Herman Hesse's celebrated novel *Steppenwolf*, one of the three novels for which Hesse was awarded the Nobel prize.

Sidis and his fictional counterpart Haller are almost identical twins, though *Steppenwolf* appeared in Germany two years after the Follupian treatise on transfers was published (1926).

Who was Harry Haller? Hesse wrote in his novel:

> There was once a man, Harry, called the Steppenwolf. He walked on two legs, wore clothes, but never-the-less, he was in reality a wolf of the Steppes.
>
> The Steppenwolf stood entirely alone outside the world of convention, since he had neither family life nor social ambitions. He felt himself to be single and alone, as a hermit, a person removed from the common run of men by the prerogative of talents that had something of genius in them.
>
> He was brought up by devoted but severe and very pious parents and teachers in accordance with the doctrine that makes the breaking of the will the cornerstone of education and upbringing. But in this case the attempt to destroy the personality and to break the will did not succeed. He was much too strong and hardy, too proud and spirited. Instead of destroying his personality, they only succeeded in teaching him to hate himself. It was against himself, innocent and noble as he was, that he directed during his life the whole wealth of his fancy, the whole of his thought; and in so far as he loosed upon himself every barbed criticism, every anger and hate he could command, he was a real Christian and a real martyr. His whole life was an example that "love of one's neighbors" is not possible without love of oneself, and that self-hate is really the same as sheer

egoism, and in the long run breeds the same cruel isolation and despair.

Herman Hesse added: "Harry Haller's sickness of the soul is *not* the eccentricity of a single individual, not the pathological fancy of an isolated temperament. I see it as a sickness of the times, the neurosis of that generation to which Haller belongs, a sickness that attacks not only the worthless and weak, but those who are strongest in spirits and richest in talents."

Recently while reading the diaries of Franz Kafka, I found an uncanny corroboration of Hesse's sociological diagnosis of Haller's "sickness of the soul." *At the very same time* that young William James Sidis was acting out his weird Harvard-streetcar-father drama, Kafka—who also believed he was being psychically murdered by his father—recorded a dream with exactly the same elements:

> May 6, 1912. I [dreamed] I was riding with my father through Berlin in a trolley. The big-city quality was represented by countless toll bars standing upright, finished off bluntly at the ends. Aside from that, almost everything was empty. But there was a great forest of these bars. We came to a gate, got out without any sense of getting out, stepped through the gate. On the other side of the gate a sheer wall rose up, which my father ascended almost in a dance. His legs flew out as he climbed, so easy was it for him. There was also some inconsiderateness in the fact that he did not help me one bit, for I got to the top only with the utmost effort, on all fours, often sliding back, as though the wall had become steeper under me. At the same time, it was also distressing that the wall was covered with human excrement so that pieces of it clung to me, chiefly to my breast. I looked down

at the pieces of shit with bowed head and ran my hand over them.

The dream ends with an account of their arrival at a university, his father's pleasure upon entering a professor's office, Kafka's unhappiness in the university environment, and his inability to respond to the pretty secretary of the professor they are visiting.

"Father," "streetcar," "university," "professor,"—every element in the humiliation of a small boy in transatlantic Boston during the year 1912—is reproduced in the resonant dream of Franz Kafka. It gives one occulistic pause.

Also, while Sidis, abandoning establishment intellectual values, was prowling the streets of Boston in search of discarded streetcar transfers, another man in Hanover, Germany, was doing the very same thing. He was the dadaist *collagist* Kurt Schwitters. But unlike the completely isolated Sidis, Schwitters was part of an organized intellectual art movement which deliberately set out to prove that the discarded cultural debris of society was more valuable than its loftiest formulations. Similarly, in 1913, when James Joyce began to write his great *Ulysses,* he asked his family in Dublin to send him all sorts of printed trivia, including streetcar trivia.

Haller and Sidis, one fictional and the other living within a fiction, are extreme examples of the alienated Outsider. But, though the resemblance between the two is uncanny, it goes much deeper than their confessed lycanthropy. Both men, I discovered, staged private passion plays in the hidden theaters of their imagination, and both revealed the existence of these theaters in their books.

When Harry Haller disappears from his boarding house he leaves behind a "Treatise on the Steppenwolf," in which he has written that one day while he was walking in the street he discovered the entrance to a "Magic Theater—not for everybody—for madmen only—price of admission your mind." It was a theater visible only to him. The rest of *Steppenwolf* describes what happens when Haller enters the theater and meets the vicious aspects of himself, both male and female, and how he acts out his destructive fantasies with them on the stage of his accelerating madness.

Sidis also left behind his treatise on peridromophily, his own word, meaning a "love of finding one's way about." In his book and in his bulletin, *The Peridromophile,* he left a definite clue to the existence and location of his own secret theater of memory. Like everything else in the mythical municipality that Sidis inhabited, his "magic" theater could be reached only on the haunted streetcar lines of which he held the exclusive franchise. And, consistent with the purity of his monomania, his theater was actually a streetcar.

My authority for this analysis is Sidis himself, and is contained in a highly compressed Kafkaesque anecdote—one of the parables scattered at random through his writings on transfers:

> A man once took his wife to the theater, and in coming downtown had to change streetcars. On reaching the theater, he presented the tickets, but was told by the doorman that they were streetcar tickets, not theater tickets. At which the man answered: "Now I know why the conductor on that second car was so pleased!"

This story of the absurd is truly absurd. Theater tickets and streetcar transfers do not in the least resemble each other, yet the absentminded "man" of the story (absent-minded Professor Sidis?) makes the same impossible mistake twice.

The "mistake" was deliberate on the part of William James Sidis. The first time it magically transformed the drab streetcar into a theater, and the dishonest streetcar conductor agrees to the Cinderella change by accepting the theater tickets in lieu of payment for the ride on his trolley. But the doorman of the theater challenged the validity of the streetcar transfers as admission to his theater. As we shall see, Sidis allowed no one to enter his theater, especially that particular man and his wife.

In this detail of his secret metaphor of revenge, Sidis, unknowingly perhaps, imitated "mad" Ludwig II of Bavaria, who once ordered a major Wagnerian opera performed for himself alone in his huge opera house.

The streetcar theater of memory constructed by Sidis had an enormous stage—exactly as big as Boston when he was a child—but its auditorium was tiny, big enough to hold only one very uncomfortable chair, a hate-and-love seat built for one, Sidis himself.

What was the nature of the performance up on the stage of the fantasy theater? Only *one* drama was ever played for its spellbound audience of one. It had no beginning and no end but ran continuously. It consisted entirely of disconnected little jokes. I have arranged all Sidis' jokes in chronological sequence, however, and have restaged the play under the title *The Streetcar Named Paradise Lost.* Like all other plays in the theater of the absurd, this one (expressed in astonishingly modern terms thirty years before Samuel

Beckett and Eugene Ionesco) invites the spectator to make up his own titles and interpretations as he rides along on the haunted streetcar.

The action takes place mainly on a Boston-to-Cambridge streetcar between the year 1902, when the infant prodigy was four years old, and 1910, when he had his first breakdown and was transferred from Harvard University to his father's mental institution in Portsmouth, New Hampshire.

There are only three characters in *The Streetcar Named Paradise Lost*. They are a little boy, obviously Willy Sidis, who is the protagonist; the Conductor (antagonist); and the Mother (sort of Greek chorus). But the Mother appears in only a few scenes that show her as weak, passive, and quite unaware of the developing drama. Occasionally, one catches a glimpse of the motorman and some other passengers, but they are merely cardboard figures.

The leading character is the Conductor. He appears in almost every scene. He is the Master of the streetcar and collects fares, making sure that everyone pays for his ride, especially little boys who try to ride for half fare. The Conductor is the villain of the play, who holds the little boy captive and delivers him every day to Harvard University.

You have already guessed who the Conductor is: Professor Boris Sidis, who first personally conducted his little genius to Harvard but then, as the boy grew older, turned him over to the conductor on the streetcar.

Here in William James Sidis' own words, we learn about the Conductor—and something else beside:

> One man said to another: "My father was an American, and my mother was an American, so that makes me an American."
>
> And the man to whom he explained this point of citizenship had the nerve to reply: "If *my father was a conductor,* and my mother was a conductorette, then *I suppose that I could be a transfer.*" [my italics]

This joke sheds bright light on the one about the college boy who attacked a policeman in the subway car in the mistaken belief that he was a conductor. ("That was no conductor I was attacking; that was my father!")

But what is most remarkable is that Sidis, who seems to become more of a character from mythology with every passing minute, is also saying, "I am a *transfer* born of a conductor and his wife." First, Sidis took the self-abasing name Frank Folupa. Now he seems to be telling us that he is a worthless piece of paper.

The confession of Sidis—"I am a transfer"—sounds mad, yet it is at the very heart of his purloined letter to the world. According to the bitter "joke," Sidis was conceived as a transfer by his conductor father and his conductorette mother. A transfer was born when the conductor took one from his virgin pad and punched it. By issuing the transfer the Conductor made it possible for the passenger to ride on a predestined route. The passenger, of course, could get off the streetcar at any point along the line, but he could not go beyond the final destination, usually the city limits. The godlike Conductor also determined the life span of the transfer by punching the exact minute of its expiration. And, conversely, he collected transfers, examined them for "signs of life," and rejected any transfer that had expired.

Again our imagery comes from Sidis. The conception of a transfer as a breathing, living person is contained in the following "quickie" from *The Peridromophile*. In this three-character scene, we see Professor Sidis, Mrs. Sidis, and a transfer named Willy.

> CONDUCTOR: This transfer has expired, madam.
> LADY: I don't blame it a bit. This streetcar is so poorly ventilated.

This "joke" reminded me of a childhood incident and led me finally to the explanation of Sidis' obsessive collecting of streetcar transfers.

When my brother Will was 12 and I 10, my mother took us with her, as protectors, on a little errand of mercy to an aged and sick relative who lived on Woodland Avenue, a disintegrating neighborhood in Cleveland. We went into a very dilapidated apartment house, and I still remember how we clung to one another fearfully as we climbed the gloomy stairway to the top floor, where the old woman lived.

My mother did not like the old woman (nobody did) but dutifully took her turn to bring food and clean linen. Will and I had to wait in the hallway while my mother bathed the old woman. When we were allowed to enter the little room, we saw that the bed had been made and that my mother was feeding the old woman soup. She was obviously dying (she did die a week later), but she still had the strength to complain bitterly about various people. I didn't understand all the rapid Yiddish of their conversation, but I noticed that my mother was quite upset and embarrassed by some of the things said by the old woman in our presence.

Will and I were also upset and frightened, and we

tried to distract ourselves by looking around the room. The old woman was well known as a recluse and a "miser," and now we saw what she did with the old broken skates and dolls, damaged crockery, and other things that she had picked up in the streets. They were all neatly arranged on the few pieces of furniture in the room.

We saw a cracked cut-glass dish with some glass marbles in it on her bureau. Will and I each picked one up and looked idly at it. From her bed the dying woman had been watching us anxiously. When she saw us pick up the marbles, she said piteously: "Please don't touch them. I *need* them."

Later, as we were descending the stairs, my mother was still very upset and said angrily: "Marbles! Where she is going she's not going to play marbles!" Then, aghast, she stopped and apologized to us: "That was a horrible, mean thing I just said about the poor old woman. She can't help herself. She has no one any more. Living alone has made her the way she is. Her whole life is in the trash she picks up in the street. Maybe she thought that if you took her marbles, she would die."

Now, four decades later, I know what my mother meant, what went on in that little room. By denying a few marbles to two children who visited her, the woman felt that she had managed to prolong her life by a few days.

It seems that a similar feeling motivated the adult Sidis in his strange quest for paper ephemera. He spent all his nonworking hours looking for abandoned pieces of paper. He traveled far and wide to his favorite transfer points, where he knew that people would throw the things away. He hung around railroad terminals on the off-chance that incoming passengers would bring in and discard transfers from distant cities. And then, with his street cleaner's "paper stabber," he would poke obsessively, anxiously, among filthy accumulations of wind-blown paper in vacant lots—an ignoble Captain Ahab harpooning little paper sperm whales!

The thin sharp nail at the end of his broomstick did little harm to the transfers, and the new punched holes as I will explain) gave additional life to the transfers.

A woman who knew Sidis in 1928 but who prefers not to be named told me: "Of course he had to use a nail-on-a stick for picking them up. He was like Humpty Dumpty—so fat that he couldn't bend over." After 39 years the sharp edge of her voice still conveyed a woman's exasperation and contempt, for a man who refused to be domesticated, who behaved like a disgusting child.

Sidis was fully aware of the abnormality of his quest. In one of his monthly bulletins (1928) he made the breezy little announcement:

"Scummy Transfers," a tale of the derelict transfers reclaimed from the street, will be printed in next month's issue of *Dirty Stories.*

Dirty Stories was a pornographic pulp magazine of the 1920s. If we read him correctly, Sidis is confessing that his penchant for rescuing soiled derelict transfers is associated with an unspecific sexual dirtiness of some kind.

Obviously, Sidis did not think of himself in highfaluting literary terms; in his own mind, he was no Melvillean Captain Ahab of the city pavements. He could draw quite well, and he created a cartoon character clearly based on himself (for the *Peridromo-*

phile) whom he called "General Phorm," a pun meaning "General form" or "ordinary transfer."

General Phorm, a transfer, is the lightly disguised knight-errant alter-ego of Sidis. Armed with a paper-stabber, he works around the clock rescuing transfers in distress. He is an exact copy of the cartoon strip character Mutt (of Mutt & Jeff) and behaves in the same infantile way. In one cartoon, for example, General Phorm is faced with a problem, one that recapitulates the father-son syndrome. A large burly man is standing on a street-corner waiting for a trolley. His left foot is on a transfer. General Phorm wants the transfer, but is afraid to ask the man to move his foot. Instead, we are told, General Phorm waits for more than 30 minutes for the streetcar to come along. (Mutt and Jeff are among the leading characters in *Finnegans Wake,* James Joyce's great cryptogram of the human condition. In this last work of Joyce's, Mutt and Jeff are grown men who are emotionally infantile and totally unable to cope with the problems they face in the adult world.)

Whenever he rescued a free transfer, Sidis rescued himself. He imagined that his father, an ogre in a fairy tale, had transformed him into a mere piece of paper and given him away freely to strangers. His desperation came from this rejection and his knowledge of the fate that befalls all transfers. Those that were used would be gathered and burned or sold for old paper and eventually reincarnated in pulp paper. Strangers tore them to bits, or tossed them in garbage and refuse containers and the transfers were washed down gutters into sewers, or left to rot and bleach in paper hells.

In his chapter "Derelict Transfers" (the term was

coined by Sidis and used only by him), he offers some hints on retrieval of these enchanted objects. When these "useful hints" are read with an awareness of his self-abasement, they seem very moving.

> The collector picking up derelicts should be as inconspicuous as possible, and should not let it be noticed what he is doing. Although picking up a derelict for a souvenir is a perfectly legitimate action in itself, still it would hardly do to appear as one who picks up rubbish, or especially one who is trying to pick up transfers to evade the payment of carfare.
>
> Wet transfers are often found adhering to the pavement, and there is special care needed to avoid tearing them, especially if there is already a slight tear. Sometimes the process of detaching such transfers can be done effectively with the point of an umbrella, which can also be used to pick up the transfer if handled properly.
>
> Snow will frequently keep transfers frozen all winter long, and many derelict transfers can be found under a deep layer of snow. When removed from the snow, these transfers may be treated essentially the same as ordinary wet transfers. But great care should be used if they have to be taken out of ice, in which case it is better to break off the whole piece of ice surrounding the transfer and let it melt.

Sidis rehabilitated his paper treasures and gave them greater value than they had ever had by making them part of his elaborately structured world of streetcar technics. He used all his high intelligence to effect the resurrection and transfiguration of the rejected and expired transfers.

After Sidis recovered his derelict transfers he continued to make endless variations and fugues on the words relating to his furious hobby. First, he shifted the word "transfer" to its other meaning as "the conveyance of a property by means of a document." Then he shifted the word "derelict" to its legal meaning: "to forsake wholly," "to abandon," a "thing cast away by its rightful owner or guardian without any intention of ever retaking it."

Anyone else would simply have picked up the damned trivia and thought nothing of it. But not Sidis. To him it was of crucial importance that each derelict transfer (himself) should belong to him *legally.*

Four times in his book Sidis warns the reader that it is illegal to collect transfers. Ted Frankel gave me a number of transfers that Sidis had given him in 1928, and every one of them carried a legal threat:

PENALTY FOR FRAUDULENT USE

It is a misdemeanor punishable by FINE not to exceed $25.00 for any person
(1) To sell, exchange, or give away this transfer.
(2) To throw away this transfer without tearing same in two.

Of course riders paid no attention to these unenforceable laws. They gave their transfers away freely, especially to schoolchildren. But to Sidis, who played his fantastic transfer game as if his life depended on it, these legal restrictions were of crucial importance. Every detail printed on a transfer can be read as a detail in his psychological life.

After Sidis rescued his transfers he made them his property by invoking the laws relating to the salvage of maritime derelicts. He then immediately abrogated the action of the Conductor who had mercilcssly assigned a half-day life span to each of them. In his collection they became timeless and eternal.

The transfers could be used to travel forward in

time, or, reversibly, they could be used for rides to the past. As such, they became lifetime tickets of admission to Sidis' private streetcar theater of memory.

At first, the little genius in *The Streetcar Named Paradise Lost* rode happily and without paying more than any other young child. Then the Conductor began to look suspiciously at him and to ask him his age. Many of the little scenes enacted in the theater-streetcar involve the attempts of little Sidis to avoid the paying of full fare:

> Mother's friends: How old are you, Percy?
> Sonny: I am four years old on the streetcar, five years old at school, and six years old at home.
>
> Do you know what happens to little boys who tell lies?
> Sure, they ride half-fare.

Here is a pithy epigram from *The Peridromophile:*

> Bad Memory may be Troublesome,
> But sometimes it pays dividends.
> As when Junior forgets how old he
> Really is on the street platform.

All these scenes seem innocent enough, but they all tell the same story: The Conductor is asking the little boy genius to pay *full fare* for his rides to Harvard. He is asking him to be mature long before he is ready, to give up his childhood as payment for being made into a superman by his father. But the little boy cannot do it, so he lies and pretends to be very stupid, as he does in a scene played with his father:

> Overheard on a Boston trolley:
> Small boy: Is this a bread train?
> Father: No.

Son: Then what is that bread doing there?
(The boy was pointing to a bread advertisement featuring a magnified picture of the loaf.)

The streetcar theater glides silently along. Weeks pass and then months. The captive child is taken to Harvard every day. He is riding to his Humpty Dumpty fall as the demands on him become unbearable. But he realizes with helpless dismay that the Conductor is indifferent to his fate, as he is to the fate of all the passengers on the streetcar.

As if to stress the fact that there is no room for love on that streetcar, little Willy tells another joke. It is rush hour, and the car is filled. The car comes to a stop, and a young couple comes aboard.

Young man: Do you think that we can squeeze in here?
Girl companion: Oh, Jay! I'd rather wait until we get home!

The next scene played on the streetcar illustrates the son's idea that the Conductor is not only indifferent to the fate of his passengers but is also a senseles brute:

A chink named Ching Ling
Fell off the streetcar. BING! BING!
The con turned his head,
To the passengers said:
The car's lost a washer, DING! DING!

And, in the same vein:

Once a prizefighter quit the ring to become a streetcar conductor. But bad habits do not wear off easily; so, whenever the motorman would start ringing the bell, the conductor would start punching all the passengers—until the bell rang again.

Little Willy Sidis then recites a couple of jokes expressing his fantasies of reprisal:

> Riddle: Why does lightning never strike the front end of a car?
> Answer: Because the motorman is not a conductor!

In one joke the Professor even becomes a streetcar:

> A scholarly and polite gentleman was walking down a slippery hill. His feet flew out from under him, and on the way down he collided with a woman, and she slid down the hill on top of him.
>
> At the bottom of the hill he said politely, "You'll have to get off here. This is as far as I go."

Willy tells another story in which a champion arises to outwit the Conductor:

> In a back country district, a notary public took a "wild-cat" interurban streetcar between towns and on getting off was informed that the fare would be two dollars.
> Notary: Do you solemnly swear that two dollars is the regular fare for this ride?
> Conductor: I do.
> Whereat, the notary paid the Conductor a dollar, stating that he was keeping the other dollar as a notary fee for administering the oath.

The little eruption of lighthearted jokes and wisecracks subsides, and the streetcar continues its single track to trouble. Some ominous notes are sounded in a single line:

> Overheard on the Boston streetcar during the 6 p.m. rush hour:
> "We are in a jam. Heaven preserve us!"

There is no escape from the Conductor, not even in death: "A man died and went to heaven, but when he got there he was told that he would have to go to the other place. Whereupon he said: 'Gimme a transfer!' "

Willy is telling us that, even when he dies and goes to heaven, we will have to face a Conductor at the Pearly Gates. But if *he* is there, Willy prefers to go to hell. Once again we have a confrontation right out of *Paradise Lost,* in the form of a tiny challenge to an unchallengeable judge—and with the same results: A little boy expelled from heaven and fallen from grace.

Then the climactic scene of *The Streetcar Named Paradise Lost* is played. Willy realized that there is a possible escape from his terrible predicament. It is really so simple! He has noticed that many other people who ride the same streetcar do not have to share his punishment. They go to other places. The magic ticket to other places is a transfer given to them by the Conductor.

Sidis stages the climactic scene in his usual bland, undramatic way: in the form of an anecdote. But what an anecdote!

> It is said that a Harvard College student got on a streetcar, and wishing an extra ride, asked the Conductor for a transfer.
> When asked: "Where to?" he said, "Anywhere."
> The conductor winked and said: "All right, I will give you a transfer to Waverly."
>
> The student was afterwards laughed at when he told the story, and was informed that the asylum for the feeble-minded was located at Waverly.

Now, at last, we have it from Sidis himself. The entire drama expressed in one little anecdote.

"When," Sidis is saying in this story, "in utter desperation, I begged my father to release me from the situation I knew would result in my emotional collapse, when I asked him to give a transfer to some other place than Harvard, he asked me, 'Where to?' I said, 'Anywhere!' But all he did was wink sadistically and give me a transfer to his own asylum in Portsmouth, New Hampshire.

"He said to me, in effect, 'Look, either you will go to Harvard and become a great genius and prove how great my theories are—or you will go to an asylum.'

"I tried to continue at the university, but I had a breakdown. Later, after I was released from my father's asylum in Portsmouth and returned to school, I felt that I was the object of derision. Now I am a derelict."

But *The Streetcar Named Paradise Lost,* a play without a beginning or an end, has two other scenes, both anticlimactic. They link the little Willy Sidis who rode the streetcar to Harvard with the adult William James Sidis who constantly acted out his childhood.

First anticlimax:

> Signs of Spring:
> Man: What are you doing there, young feller?
> Boy: Waiting for a streetcar.
> Man: Well, you'll wait a long while, that line only runs in the summer.

Perhaps the saddest story left behind by the vanished Sidis was the second of the anticlimactic scenes from the streetcar theater of his memory:

> A man was seen walking a car track—an old, abandoned line—and gazing intently at the rails. A bystander called out to him:
> "Hey, what are you doing there?"

"Why, I'm a detective!"
"What are you looking for?"
"The president of the streetcar company."
"Well, you don't expect to find him here, do you?"
"No, but I'm on his track, anyhow."

So ends the mythical drama of *The Streetcar Named Paradise Lost.* I had hoped to find and present a more conclusive ending to the story, but we know that the life of William James Sidis ended abruptly in 1944, when he died of pneumonia.

I am an incurable romantic. Someday, somehow, I hope to find the missing last scene of our *Paradise Lost* drama, and when I do I hope it plays as follows:

"One day William James Sidis finds *the* transfer that he has always been looking for. He finds it embedded in a block of clear ice (his own wonderful poetic image), and it reads, *Boston Street R.R.—Paradise Lost Line.* With that transfer William James Sidis enters his magic theater, walks onto the stage, and jumps onto the moving streetcar marked "Paradise Lost." As he jumps he is magically transformed back into his twelve-year-old self in the year 1910. Little Willy Sidis walks up to the Conductor and hands him the transfer that he has just found.

WILLY SIDIS: Gimme a transfer.
PROFESSOR SIDIS: Where to?
SON: You know where to. Hand it over!
FATHER: Yes, son.

The Professor takes an unused pad of transfers from his leather pouch, tears one off, punches it, and hands it to his son. Father and son ride along on the silent streetcar for a few minutes. Then the car stops at a transfer point, and Willy Sidis leaps off without a backward glance. He walks a few steps and boards the waiting streetcar marked "Paradise Regained." On that trolley he rides to a suburb of Boston that he has never seen before. There he finds his lost childhood."

Now let me tell you the real ending. Some months ago I went to the New York Public Library to look for Sidis material. I walked bravely past the stone lions that guard the building, up the stairs and past the huge painting of John Milton dictating *Paradise Lost* to his daughters and then to the main catalogue room on the third floor.

In the catalogue room I looked for the drawer containing the file card for *Notes on the Collection of Transfers* under the pseudonym Frank Folupa, but I saw that the librarians had brushed aside the pseudonym and had catalogued the book under the author's real name: "See *Sidis*, William James."

I walked over to the drawer marked "Sickle-Sidm" and found the card for "William James Sidis, *Notes on the Collection of Transfers*" right next to the file cards for the six books written by Professor Boris Sidis.

There they were—Father and Son—on adjacent white cards, perfectly punched and in exact alignment, neatly impaled on a common steel rod.

The card for *Notes on the Collection of Transfers* is cheek to cheek with *Studies in Multiple Personality, Philistine or Genius?*, and *The Psychology of Laughter*.

At last Professor Boris Sidis and his Prodigal Son Willy are reunited, in a comfortable steel drawer in the main catalogue room of the New York Public Library, where they will snuggle together for all bibliographical eternity.

Who is Santa Claus?

Every Christmas Eve, the mysterious Falstaffian familiar—known to others as Sinterklaas, Père Noël, Kris Kringle, Saint Nicholas, or Father Christmas but to us as Santa Claus—makes his regular nonscheduled flight to this country in his reindeer-drawn aerial sleigh. He glides bliplessly and undetected through the supervigilant Early Warning System and arrives simultaneously in every locality in the United States, including Hawaii and Alaska. Then, during the very short winter's night, Santa Claus unerringly delivers nearly $2 billion worth of individually selected gifts to about 40 million sleeping children.

The entire amazing operation is performed flawlessly with *Rififi*-like stealth and cool, while Santa Claus, nicely described by the Dutch psychoanalyst Adriaan de Groot as the "Secret Donor par excellence," remains invisible, speaks to no one, and never waits for expressions of delight or gratitude.

After completing his miracle of discreet philanthropy, the transcendental Phileas Fogg leaps into his sleigh at precisely the crack of dawn on Christmas Day (6:57 a.m.). The well-known Dancer, Prancer, Donder, Blitzen, and company then whisk him home with the speed of light to his factory-warehouse complex at the North Pole, and he plunges at once (6:58 a.m.) into planning and production for the following Christmas.

As with so many of the things that are most immediate to our lives, this prodigious Secret Donor remains shrouded in mystery. Out of what dim, half-forgotten ages does he come, and what rare ingredients went into the making of his indestructible being? But one question must be asked about him that is far more important, far more intriguing, than any other. Why is it that, year after year, millions of American families invite this shadowy figure into their homes, onto their very hearths, to be the instrument of their clandestine Christmas giving? Answer that, and you have come close to solving the question of who and what is Santa Claus.

After many years of cynical indifference, I regained my childhood belief in Santa Claus—and began to sense the profundity of his actions—while I was visiting Bari, an old seaport on Italy's Adriatic coast. Although they happened exactly twenty years ago, I still remember clearly the incidents that led me to an investigation of the strange career of our elusive nocturnal benefactor.

As I wandered through the lovely neglected old town with its once-famous harbor (Julius Caesar, Brutus, Tiberius, and Pontius Pilate sailed to Egypt and the Holy Land from Barium), a curious thing happened. I am an art buff and collector of popular folk art and always carefully study such objects wherever I go. But in Bari on that particular morning the process reversed itself. I had the uneasy sensation that the bishop in two dramas I saw depicted everywhere was studying *me*. Every restaurant, every shop, every outdoor shrine displayed an image of at least one of these surrealistic dramas, and, always, the sad-looking bishop was the leading actor.

In one painted happening, the mitered bishop,

though always dressed in the resplendent robes of his office, was not in his cathedral performing a High Mass. Instead, he was standing in a humble butcher shop before a large barrel, out of which three naked boys had sprung.

The second of the haunting images was even more enigmatic, disquieting, and even poetic. In it it is always the middle of the night. The streets of a medieval village are deserted except for the melancholy bishop, who stands alone outside the window of a bedroom. Inside, three young girls are asleep in the same narrow bed, and near them is an ugly old man. Sometimes the old man is asleep, but at other times he is depicted as insomniacally seated on a chair. Is this evil-looking man the father of the girls or their captor? He cannot see the bishop, who, in every version of the scene, is *surreptitiously* throwing a moneybag through the window into the room.

The mild delusion of mysterious pursuit, incited by the constant appearance of these pictures, reached a kind of climax at 11:15 one morning. I entered a small café and found not one but both icons ornately framed under fly-specked glass, pretending they had been there long before my arrival.

There was only one thing to do: I asked the café owner and his waiter to tell me about the pictures. They were surprised and delighted by a foreigner's interest in their private icons and sailed into an excited and literal reenactment of the scenes. It was charming and funny but not very helpful.

I thought that I understood their redundant pantomime but could get only the following facts from their high-speed explanations: The bishop was San Nicola. He was the local patron saint. These pictures showed his two most important miracles. His "holy bones" were in the Basilica of San Nicola near the center of town. If I hurried, I could get there before it closed for the afternoon.

At the basilica there was no guide in sight to show me the tomb. Suddenly a new mystery popped up from the floor; there were Arabic words woven through the intricate design of the circular border all around the altar! Similar mosaics in other parts of the Mediterranean came to mind, and I assumed that, like the others, this tessellated floor and its intrusive Arabic calligraphy had been installed during a Muslim occupation of Bari in the fourteenth or fifteenth century.

My assumption was wrong. As I stared at the wall-to-wall mystery, a pale, uniformed guide materialized. "Excuse me, sir," he said cheerfully, "but I see that you are admiring our *pavimento*. You are thinking—as all visitors do—that they were placed here by Muhammadan invaders."

"I guess I *was* thinking that. But in other places—"

He interrupted. "*Other places* were occupied by the Moors. But never Bari! These words were placed here by Moorish artists brought from Sicily. When they realized that our holy fathers could not read Arabic, the infidels put their creed—'There is no God but Allah, and Muhammad is his prophet!'—in many parts of the basilica."

"Why weren't the words removed later on?"

"It would have been impossible without ruining the whole floor. Besides, none of the common people realized these were Arabic words. Until very recently, most of them couldn't even read Italian. And now"—he shrugged—"it doesn't matter."

As I continued to gaze in admiration at what was perhaps the most exquisite practical joke in history—or was it a poineer act of ecumenism?—the guide abruptly changed the subject: "But, sir, you are an American! You did not come so far to read Arabic from a mosaic *pavimento*. You came to see San Nicola. You came to see Saint Nicholas! You came to see Santa Clothes! Come, I will show you Santa Clothes!"

Santa Claus! Was this—this *foreigner* trying to tell me that the sad-looking, *skinny* local saint was actually our American Santa Claus?

That is exactly what he was telling me. "San Nicola was originally called Saint Nicholas of Myra, an ancient seaport in Asia Minor, near the island of Rhodes," he began. "He was buried there until 1087. At that time, some Barese sailors heard their Venetian rivals were going to make a raid on Myra to liberate the body of Saint Nicholas from the Turkish infidels. But our sailors got there first and brought the body here."

He then explained that San Nicola is honored only on his birthday (December 6) and has no connection with the Italian celebration of Christmas. The only traditional Italian folk figure resembling our Santa Claus is a little old woman called Befana. She gets her name from Epiphany, because she comes on January 6, the Day of Epiphany, when the Wise Men visited the Manger. Befana rides a broomstick, comes down the chimney, and gives presents only to good children. Bad children find ashes, pieces of coal, and rusty nails in their stockings.

At first, my interest in Saint Nicholas was merely incidental to a general preoccupation with folklore. But after some research and iconographic study it became more and more apparent that this mythical saint (as of 1969, the Roman Catholic Church doubts that he ever existed, and he has been dropped from the Church calendar, along with such notables as Saint Christopher, Saint Valentine, and Saint Patrick) was different from all other saints. He was credited with miracles that became more and more profound as one thought about them.

The legendary Nicholas was born in the fourth century in Asia Minor (now Turkey) of wealthy Greek parents. At birth he astonished—and frightened—the midwives by standing bolt upright during his very first bath and for two full hours afterward, a record for a newborn infant that has remained unchallenged for sixteen centuries.

His parents and their awestruck neighbors naturally enough regarded this extraordinary feat as a miracle, and, when the infant adamantly refused to accept more than one breast feeding on Wednesdays and Fridays (because they were fast days), all were convinced that Nicholas was predestined for sainthood.

Nicholas' entire life was filled with such theatrical miracles. When, for example, the old Bishop of Myra died, it was decided that his successor should be chosen magically. The first male who entered the cathedral on a secretly designated day would be named the new bishop. Early one morning, the selection committee waited inside the cathedral for the door to open, and I'll bet you'll never guess who walked in!

From the beginning, Saint Nicholas was the patron of all the people. He became the protector of shipwrecked sailors and other men, including pawnbrokers and thieves, who worked in hazardous trades. But mainly he was the guardian saint of young children and of girls without dowries, and it was for them that he performed most of his innumerable miracles.

But always—and this is for me the heart of the Saint Nicholas—Santa Claus legend—the saint performed his rescues in a manner that makes one think he was a predecessor of Dr. Sigmund Freud. A farfetched comparison? Perhaps. But let's look at the two miracles of Saint Nicholas that I saw depicted everywhere in Bari and then decide whether or not it is farfetched.

The Miracle of the Three Sleeping Girls. In this early Christian story, Saint Nicholas established the moral and psychological patterns, as well as the modus operandi, for all his miraculous actions. Late one night, the ancient story goes, Saint Nicholas sensed that somewhere in the city a terrible crime was about to be committed. He arrived magically at the home of an evil nobleman who had become impoverished and could not provide the all-important dowries for his three virgin daughters. The man was preparing to sell the girls to a house of prostitution the following morning.

Saint Nicholas, without permitting himself to be seen, threw a bag of gold into the room and then disappeared. He repeated this act on successive nights, to make sure that the evil father would use the money for its intended purpose. On the third night, the identity of the family's benefactor became known, for the father hid outside and saw the Bishop in action. The father seized Saint Nicholas, thanked him, and begged forgiveness for his intended crime. After a meaningful delay, Saint Nicholas forgave the filthy man. The pattern of happy endings for all Saint Nicholas stories is established here: The girls are saved from a life of shame, they find good husbands, and the father is rehabilitated.

The Miracle of the Butcher Shop. While preparing to officiate at mass, Saint Nicholas divined that a hideous crime was being enacted against innocent people. He instructed his clergymen to carry on and left the church. Guided by his mystical extrasensory powers, he arrived at a butcher shop owned by a pagan.

Saint Nicholas entered, walked unerringly to one of the many barrels in the shop, and raised his hand in benediction. At once the pieces of meat in the barrel reassembled, and three naked boys, who had been murdered by the butcher and were about to be sold as pork, leaped out of the barrel and danced joyously about the Bishop. In some of the icons of this tale, the cannibalistic butcher begs for mercy. Once again, after a curious bit of moral strategy in which Saint Nicholas hesitates, he forgives the dreadful man. (I would have clubbed him!)

Two other legends attached to the life of Nicholas must be examined before we can fully understand the meanings of all his acts.

The Miracle of the Boiled Bambino. In this fable, a young mother, preparing to bathe her child, places him in a metal tub and begins to heat the water by lighting a fire under it. Then the desperately forgetful woman runs off to church to light candles to her favorite saint, Nicholas. With the speed of light, Saint Nicholas flies to the woman's house, gets there in the (Saint) nick of time (possible origin of the phrase), and snatches the baby from death. The mother begs forgiveness, and Saint Nicholas grants it.

The Miracle of the Condemned Prisoners. Three innocent men are condemned to death as the result of an enemy's perjured testimony. Saint Nicholas arrives just as the axes are about to fall and confronts the perjurer. He confesses, and the prisoners are released and returned to their families. With his characteristic generosity, Saint Nicholas forgives the guilty man.

The tipoff to the mythical nature of these stories, if such a hint is required, is their "threeness." The three boys, three daughters, and three bags of gold recall at once the patterns of the fairy tales we all read as children: three kings, three sons, three princesses, three wishes, three little pigs, and even the three companions of little Dorothy in *The Wizard of Oz.*

But what do these stories tell us about the role Saint Nicholas has played in the lives of hundreds of millions of people through the ages? For it would be naïve to dismiss the legends as mere tales without meaning.

It is clear at once that they reveal three important aspects of Saint Nicholas' mythical character. In the first place, their persistence of these tales through so many centuries tells us that they have fulfilled a desperate yearning among the expendable common people for a supernatural friend at court, a divine ombudsman, who could bring direct help to individuals in dire need.

Second, the saint has been a kind of grand private eye, a divine detective who works invisibly to ferret out crimes that have been or are about to be committed against the innocent. Arriving magically at the scene, he uses his powers to prevent the crime. When a crime has been committed, he undoes or erases it.

Finally, Saint Nicholas acts as a supreme judge-psychiatrist who loves, understands, and forgives all men, regardless of their actions. After having, in his role as detective, discovered the crime, Saint Nicholas quickly assumes this new character. In each story the criminal does not at first understand the true nature of the sleuth who has found him out and assumes that Saint Nicholas, like every other authority figure he has known, will punish him. He therefore begs for mercy.

It is at this point that the supernatural aspect of the Saint Nicholas stories yields to the saint's assumption of the role of a modern psychoanalyst toward the culprit. Saint Nicholas does not scold, threaten, or punish. Instead he silently listens to the sinner's frightened plea for clemency and conveys a feeling that he loves and understands him, despite his stupid, cruel, or murderous intentions.

In these pre-Freudian dramas, the entire process of psychotherapy, which can in fact take years, is compressed into a few minutes. For the saint's love and understanding and his refusal to punish have an instant rehabilitating effect upon the culprit. They dissolve the hard core of evil that made his crimes necessary. At this point, the criminal changes his plea for mercy to a plea for forgiveness. But Saint Nicholas, pioneer Freudian that he is, still remains silent, and soon the guilty person realizes that he must understand himself, judge himself, forgive himself. When Saint Nicholas observes that the criminal has, in effect, rehabilitated himself, he too forgives him.

"Before the tenth century," de Groot has written, "Saint Nicholas became greater than all the saints and was called 'the second Saviour' because of his Christ-like forgiveness of all men." But his virtues were his undoing. After the Reformation Saint Nicholas was quickly discarded by the Protestants. They believed in direct access to God and no longer wanted saints to act as intermediaries. And so Saint Nicholas disappeared from much of Europe and North America for a little over two hundred years. But the world still needed his special therapeutic services, and he was eventually resurrected under a variety of disguises and pseudonyms.

In England, in the middle of the nineteenth century, Queen Victoria's consort, Prince Albert, introduced a folk figure named Knecht Ruppert from his native Germany and renamed him Father Christmas. He soon became the gift bringer to all little Britishers. In the United States, Washington Irving helped to rehabilitate the almost forgotten Saint Nicholas by writing stories about Sinterklaas, the rather sinister winter spirit brought to New Amsterdam by the early Dutch settlers. Sinterklaas did indeed become Santa Claus, though in Irving's version he retained many of the gnomish characteristics of his Dutch original.

Our current popular stereotype of Santa Claus was dreamed up by the American political cartoonist Thomas Nast—who also invented the Republican elephant and the Democratic donkey—in his drawings for *Harper's Weekly* during the 1880s. A close look at the generous senior citizen created by Nast reveals a close resemblance to Old King Cole (that merry old soul) divested of his crown and dressed in winter furs. Nast's conception caught the public fancy and quickly replaced all the earlier images of Santa Claus.

The triumph of Nast's rotund and warmhearted Santa represented a significant change in people's thinking. The images of Saint Nicholas found in American children's scrapbooks antedating Nast's Santa are fairly grim. Gone was the all-embracing, Christlike, divine lifeguard. He no longer rescued anyone; instead this secularized saint carried a whip in one hand and a toy in the other. And he was no longer allowed to indulge in his nocturnal habit of secret generosity; for he came in daylight and held kangaroo courts, in which he judged every child according to a merciless Victorian moral code. Like the odious Befana, he gave presents to good children and whipped the daylights out of bad ones.

But, as our country became more and more prosperous and Victorian ideas of conduct gave way to a new permissiveness, Nast's jolly Santa revealed again many of those characteristics that had once made Nicholas the most beloved saint in all Christendom. True to the formulas established by his fourth-century prototype, Santa Claus now arrives in the middle of the night to rescue the American family. He does so by acting as an invited supernatural mediator in the year-long domestic struggle waged by that Odd Couple known as parent and child.

Santa is invited because each of us is aware of how extremely difficult it is to be a child. To be forced to live in a world created and dominated by those loving, tall despots called "parents" and "adults" and to receive food and shelter and clothing and toys and entertainment and candy and guidance and love—especially love—that must be paid for item for item is very trying.

But we parents also know—or the ancient folk wisdom hidden inside social custom knows it for us—that once a year the little Oedipal stranger in our midst must be given one day of respite from the necessity of paying for all he gets. And that is why we stage the Christmas Eve charade and bring in that veteran performer named Santa Claus to be the gift giver.

Yes, I believe in Santa Claus! Not, of course, in the commercial humanoid who is endlessly reproduced during the Christmas season. I put my faith in the invisible Santa Claus, who has always been a useful myth. That is why I am grateful for the mythical reality of Santa Claus. He doesn't widen the credibility Grand Canyon more than a fraction of an inch. He comes and goes quickly. He brings a flash of gaiety and happiness to millions. And he always leaves behind a singing night cryptogram.

Decoded, the message reads: "Magical repeat magical possibility exists in universe. Stop. Yes comma possibility exists that anyone repeat anyone can learn to give love comma understanding comma and to grant amnesty to children. Stop. But must be done invisibly comma secretly comma and without expectations of a single thing in return. Stop. See you next Christmas. Stop. Love to all." Below the message is a note from the telegraph company: "Upon request of sender, signature withheld."

Albert Schweitzer

THE MAN FROM STRASBOURG

My journalistic encounter with the great Albert Schweitzer began with what seemed at the time a miracle. The notes I have saved as a souvenir of that memorable episode tell me that on the morning of July 9, 1955, in a hotel room in Stockholm, I began to read Dr. Schweitzer's autobiography and became enthralled at once by the legendary story of the 29-year-old genius who in 1904 decided to sacrifice his brilliant careers in theology, teaching, philosophy, and music to devote the rest of his long life to medical service in a remote part of French Equatorial Africa. Now the spiritually deprived world had finally become aware of the eighty-year-old missionary hero and was forcing its honors upon him. Just three years before, in 1952, Dr. Schweitzer had been awarded the Nobel Peace prize, but he did not go to Sweden to respond to the award because he was building a new clinic at Lambaréné and believed that he could not be spared. It was a wonderful, heartwarming story: For once saintliness was being rewarded by something other than neglect, martyrdom—or canonization after death.

I fell into a pleasant Thurberesque reverie in which I too had given up everything (well, almost everything), earned a degree in tropical medicine, mastered several Gabonese dialects and drum telegraphy, rejected the tinsel values of our materialistic and dissension-torn society, returned my overdue library books, and hastened to join "Ogongo, the great white wizard" in his demiparadise at Lambaréné, where all black and white men were like brothers. There, during the long, fulfilling days, I stood at the right hand of Dr. Schweitzer healing the beautiful and grateful Africans—and also the trembling, Bambi-like creatures that came limping out of the dense surrounding jungle.

But at night . . . at night I sat with the great musical doctor at his zinc-lined, termite-repelling upright piano and played duets, usually accompanied by our chronically enraged, chest-thumping neighborhood gorilla. But, just as we reached the middle of Franz Schubert's enchanting *Fantasia in F for Four Hands* (opus 103), my hotel telephone rang and broke the spell: "We have a cable for you. Shall we send it up?" A few minutes later I read the following message from an editor of *Collier's Magazine* in New York: "YOUR PHOTOSTORY SWEDEN OKAY STOP YOULL BE PLEASED NEXT ASSIGNMENT STOP PHOTOINTERVIEW DR ALBERT SCHWEITZER NOW VACATIONING HIS HOME GUNSBACH ALSACE FRANCE STOP PICKUP DETAILED LETTER INSTRUCTIONS PARIS AND TELEPHONE ME STOP BESTS."

I held the autobiography of Dr. Schweitzer in one hand and the totally unexpected cablegram in the other and immediately fell off my rather rickety "rocker"! The astonishing coincidence deranged me, and for one thrilling, goofy moment I was convinced that I controlled *Collier's Magazine* with my intercontinental (ICBM) subconscious telepathy and that the formidable editor was my helpless puppet. Obviously, when I had impulsively reached for the paperbound Schweitzer autobiography at the hotel newsstand the previous afternoon, I had magically, unwittingly, telekinetically commanded the editor to send me to "photointerview Dr. Schweitzer."

In Paris I found my instructions from *Collier's* and telephoned New York. Cables from the magazine and from an organization that helped to raise money for the famous hospital at Lambaréné were already on the way to the doctor. "But," an editor warned, "we have been advised that, though the doctor understands the value of publicity for his hospital and always cooperates with accredited writers and photographers, his possessive palace guard might set up roadblocks. If that happens try to contact him directly. If you run into trouble, let us know and we will work something from this end."

I was to drive to Gunsbach, about 250 miles northeast of Paris, and to interview Dr. Schweitzer, if he was willing, about the enormous demands made on him by the multitudes who now looked to him for guidance. In his autobiography he had written that, in addition to the staggering load of medical and administrative work at his hospital and his prolific writing on philosophical and musical subjects, he also felt bound to answer the great flood of mail that he received. Even when he returned to Europe for his periodical working "vacations," he had written, he always carried large sacks of mail to be answered in his extremely limited spare time.

We therefore hoped to elicit from him some observations on the spiritual state of the world as it was revealed to him by his international correspondents—as well as some of his answers to them. His statements were to be accompanied by color photographs of his beautiful native Alsace, familiar to me from previous photographic assignments. The photographs would illustrate the extreme differences between Dr. Schweitzer's two worlds: The compulsively tended hillsides of eastern France, all covered by good things to eat or drink, where every grapevine is neatly pruned to fit into the precise floral geometry of the region, would serve as a visul contrast to the reader's image of the riotously uncontrolled jungles in French Equatorial Africa. We would show part of Schweitzer's France, a storehouse of cultural and emotional treasures to which he came, Antaeus-like, to renew his strength—and Schweitzer's punishing Africa, to which he returned to expend himself in the service of those who desperately needed him.

I picked up a rental car and drove to northeastern France through the countryside of St. Joan of Lorraine and on to Strasbourg (where young Albert Schweitzer earned *four* doctorates at the university and where he lectured and wrote about the personality and divine mission of Jesus), then southward along the German border for about 25 miles to Colmar and neighboring Gunsbach. Gunsbach (population 500) lies in the beautiful narrow Munster Valley leading up into the high Vosges Mountains of eastern France. The region has many very beautiful medieval towns like Ricquewihr, Turckheim and Kaysersberg (Schweitzer's birthplace). But Gunsbach, a drab village built in a clumsy 19th-century German style, is interesting only for its associations with Schweitzer: the needle-spired Lutheran church, where his father was pastor for many years and where Albert began to play the organ for services when he was only nine years old; the spot on the road where Albert's mother was trampled to death by cavalry horses during World War I; the tiny cemetery where she and her husband are buried (their famous son is buried at Lambaréné), and the large residence built by the doctor.

I cruised up and down the roads of Gunsbach past Dr. Schweitzer's house in a series of slow reconnaissance passes and then decided to wait until the following day before trying to see him.

There was no hotel in Gunsbach so I drove to the nearby town of Munster and found a room at the Hôtel de la Cigogne, operated by Valentin Diebold and his sister Elizabeth, who is married to Cyril Radcliffe, a former British soldier now employed in France as a textile engineer. The hotel is named for the *cigognes* (storks) that have always wintered in Africa as far south as Capetown and summered in Europe as far north as Scandinavia, a migrational range of more than 8,000 miles. But the storks of Munster had not returned since the bombings of World War II, and their enormous rooftop nests were either empty or occupied by rather glum plaster dummies.

That evening, hoping to learn something about Dr. Schweitzer from his neighbors, I dined in the hotel restaurant on the famous specialty of the house: trout from the nearby mountain stream broiled with almonds and perfectly matched with a white Ricquewihr wine recommended by Diebold. The delicious meal was accompanied by a concert of haunting, slightly demented music from somewhere on the premises. Baffled and curious, I interrupted my meal briefly, went downstairs to investigate, and was relieved to discover that the *William Tell* Overture was being performed not by hired lunatics but by a robot string quartet and piano imprisoned behind the Biedermeier windows of a monstrous music box. The ancient *Violina* played incessantly from noon to midnight for the aperitif- and beer-drinking tourists, who gawked at its automated performances and, as I watched, even tried to dance to an excruciatingly out-of-tune cybernetic fox-trot.

A waiter told me that every two months or so a

gnomish old man, the last possessor of its arcane mechanical secrets, came down from Strasbourg to trim its horsehairs, change its catguts, remove the bat guano-like mounds of rosin dust from under the strings, and tune the instruments. But soon after he left each time, the violins and the cello would begin to go their separate ways. With each 20-franc piece deposited the gay Viennese music became more herniated until finally, in self-defense, the proprietors would snatch the machine's electric plug from the wall and put up a sign: "We regret the *Violina* is temporarily out of service, awaiting the arrival (unpredictable) of the man from Strasbourg."

As I stood captivated by this hypnotic musical monster for a few minutes, submissively throwing coins into its insatiable slot, I sensed a curious similarity between the itinerant "old man from Strasbourg" and Albert Schweitzer, who had studied, taught, preached, and maintained his medical headquarters in Strasbourg for more than sixty years. In his *Life and Thoughts* he had written that, wherever he played the pipe organ on his frequent money-raising tours, he had always felt compelled to clean, repair, and tune the church organ, which always went out of whack soon after he left.

He also described his relentless campaigns to "obtain the rescinding of death sentences that had already been passed on beautiful old organs," and he wrote jokingly, "In Africa he saves old Negroes, but in Europe old organs, my friends say of me." (The original German phrase *er errettet alte Neger* has been incorrectly translated into English [all editions] as "he saves old niggers." Several German scholars have told me that there is no German equivalent for the hateful American term "nigger." This point is mentioned at the outset to draw attention to the manner in which Dr. Schweitzer has sometimes been characterized, favorably and unfavorably, on the basis of statements mistakenly or willfully attributed to him.) Future psychoanalysts or biographers may seek and find the explanations for the curious fact that, though Albert Schweitzer unstintingly describes his own personal torments and sacrifices, he also feels it necessary to devote more than 50 pages of his short personal history to the esoteric techniques of organ playing, organ construction, and organ repair, as well as to his strenuous efforts to save the old instruments from being replaced by "plebeian factory organs." But, in the same book, he can find only 75 less than passionate words for the entire story of his wife's equal sacrifices in giving up the comforts and security of Europe to work as his first nurse in Africa, her separation from their daughter who had to stay in Europe, her frequent illnesses brought on by the rigors of jungle life, her total physical breakdown, and her permanent retirement in Europe. In fact, Schweitzer mentions his wife (Helene Bresslau Schweitzer) by name only once in his entire autobiography.

But Albert Schweitzer was no ordinary man, and it may be a mere exercise in irrelevance to apply Emily Post or even Marquis of Queensberry rules of conduct to this conscience-stricken superhero who, like Hercules or the biblical Jacob, was forced to wrestle alone with his angels and his devils. Some vicarious spectators at mankind's perpetual spiritual Olympics (that is, some history buffs) will recall that most of the great tragic heroes of religion and mythology were predestined as reluctant solo performers: Inevitably, their families, friends, disciples (and enemies) have been cast in subordinate roles. The same sagas also remind us, however, that some of the supporting actors have been well compensated for their sacrifices, humble devotion, and lesser billing. They have lived longer, become holier than thou, escaped oblivion, attained glory by association, and sometimes even hit the best-seller lists with their recollections of the fallen heroes.

Maybe, I thought, while watching the recidivist *Violina* bravely struggle through "The Blue Danube Waltz," Schweitzer's literary detours through the simpler world of organ mechanics gave him a desperately needed relief from the man-eating morality play in which he felt driven to perform and dominate stage-center at all times. I remembered that, similarly, Herman Melville stopped his dramatic story of Captain Ahab's monomaniacal hunt of the terrible white whale dead in its tracks—more than once—to digress on the anatomy, physiology, and plankton preferences of all whales.

Here are some hard questions: Did these two great spiritual adventurers interrupt their dramatic narratives because, *as writers,* they knew the value of delaying actions for the heightening of suspense? Or did they, *as men,* panic, falter, wriggle, stall, and filibuster with anticlimactic trivia when they realized the enormity of the moral tasks for which they had been shanghaied?

"The *Violina*? Dr. Schweitzaire? He was *fascinated* by the *Violina!*" Elizabeth Radcliffe told me. "Whenever he visited us during his vacations or recital tours before the war, he would listen to it—and laugh. Once he told my father, teasing him—he is a great tease sometimes: 'It is possible that the *Violina* goes out of tune *deliberately*. Maybe it wants to be chic and play dissonant contemporary music like Stravinsky and

Schönberg. Perhaps you are being unkind to your music box when you keep it playing correctly. It wants to join the modern age and you won't allow it.'

"But," she added, "it's a funny thing. The doctor still comes here sometimes with visitors when his home facilities can't handle it or when he has an important guest. But now we cover up the *Violina* when we know he is coming. It doesn't seem, well, *right* anymore. He is such a famous man now. And he seems to have forgotten it."

"Dr. Schweitzer is a vegetarian," I said, changing the subject. "What do you serve him?"

Elizabeth Radcliffe looked at her brother and smiled: "Tell him, Val, he looks like his illusions need a bit of attention." Diebold, a faintly sardonic and keenly intelligent man, was (as I had learned) still recovering from the physical effects of his terrible ordeal in a Japanese prisoner-of-war camp, but he obviously enjoyed watching the antic parade of those who came to honor the newly created nieghborhood saint. He looked me over with mock seriousness and said, "Do you think this fellow is strong enough to share our little secret?"

"I hope so," replied his sister, "but there is no danger. You can tell people anything you wish about Dr. Schweitzer. They will only believe what they came here believing."

Finally, with a little prompting, Valentin began: "Well, if you insist. We like Dr. Schweitzer very much, he is always *très gentil*, and we are proud to serve him, but there is always the same pantomime comedy. The distinguished guests arrive. They are seated. To other guests, we offer the usual menu of meat and fish. But for Dr. Schweitzer there is always ordered *the* vegetable salad. You know, lettuce and tomatoes—whatever is in season. At a certain moment the guests all look at the special salad served to the doctor, and look at him with speechless admiration because of his 'reverence for life.' Then they look down at their own food and look very guilty for a moment. But it is a short moment, and they begin to eat. Then, as the meal continues, the great man munches away on his grass and things, but everyone there knows that he is quite old and really cannot live on the stuff. A restaurant is not a meadow, and a man is not a cow. A man needs animal protein for survival and strength. So, while the doctor is talking seriously and entirely unaware of what he is eating, one of his staff, or an old friend quickly pushes a lamb chop, or something, in front of him. He doesn't see it. Nobody does. Suddenly, it disappears. Where did it go? No one knows. The lamb chop is quicker than the eye!"

On the following morning Madame Emmy Martin, Dr. Schweitzer's secretary, delivered "la brush-off téléphonique": "We have received no cables or letters from America about you. But even if we did the doctor cannot see you. He has instructed me that he has too much work to do. So there will be no interviews! No radio! No cinema! No television! No photographs! *Rien à faire!* [Nothing doing!] Sorry. Goodbye." (The sharp drop of Madame Martin's telephone on its hook instantly caused a scene from my internal film library to flash: It showed the celebrated Madame Defarge seated at the foot of a guillotine, busily knitting a neckless sweater. Up above on the platform, neatly trussed, with my head poking through the hole in the wooden thing, my last words were, "Knit me an 'extra large,' Madame Defarge, and send the bill to Robespierre.") My advance intelligence from New York had been accurate, dammit, and now I would have to yell for help and try to make contact with Dr. Schweitzer when he appeared in public.

I cabled New York immediately, wrote Dr. Schweitzer a letter explaining my presence in Gunsbach and my modest mission, translated it into proper formal German (with the kind help of Diebold and the Radcliffes); photographed Gunsbach, the old family church, and the doctor's house from every angle; and began talking with his neighbors and friends, including postman Francis Xavier Panzer. While posing for pictures with his bicycle and carrying a heavy sack of mail to the doctor's house, Panzer told me that he delivered about five thousand letters to the doctor's house annually and that the doctor himself had told him that he received another ten-to-fifteen thousand letters at Lambaréné. From the looks of the letters, said Dr. Panzer, about half were business letters and the rest personal.

The lively traffic of queen mothers, famous politicians, movie stars, tourists, artists, musicians, rich people, journalists, and camermen who came to rivet their attentions on the vacationing Ogongo delighted his neighbors in their ringside seats at the mythogenic arena. They gossiped happily about the VIPs and were amused by all the cheerful neo-Canterbury penitents who emitted ecstatic screams and blinding photoflashes whenever they spotted the great man or one of his famous visitors. But one could see that they were definitely not amused by the occasional bus loads of German civilians who placed huge wreaths at the door of the doctor's house and then lined up in military formation to bombard its walls with heavy chorales. The ambitious Teutonic songs, each requiring about fifteen minutes to reach its first thunderous climax, would ricochet through the valley and bring back memories of other days and other Germans who loved to forgather to sing "Yo! Ho! Ho!" songs when their murderous day's work was done.

Soon, to my surprise, it became apparent that public opinion in his home territory was rather cool toward Albert Schweitzer. Even those who expressed admiration for his work in Africa and his phenomenal achievement in becoming an embodiment of world conscience displayed none of the adulation reflected in a recent nationwide American poll that had selected Schweitzer—over Winston Churchill and Mahatma Gandhi—as the "most revered man of our times."

The ambivalent attitudes of his fellow Alsatians seemed to derive partly from the fact that Alsace and Lorraine, on the border between France and Germany, had been torn away from France by Bismarck in 1870 and then restored in 1918. Yet nearly forty years later Schweitzer, unlike his brother Paul, who spoke French, still preferred to speak and write in German. But what *really* infuriated them was his insistence on referring to French localities by their old German names. (I verified this point later when I lost nearly an hour trying to find a village mentioned in one of Schweitzer's books as Wir am Thal.)

"Schweitzer is a very good man," said one hot-and-cold old resident of Munster, "but sometimes he has made some unfair propaganda. In his autobiography he writes that during the 1914 war his father's church was 'damaged by *French* artillery firing from the Vosges Mountains.' But Schweitzer wasn't here. He was in a French internment camp because he was then a German citizen. But my relatives who *were* said that there was shooting from all sides. Let us say that both sides were responsible. These things happen in a war. But nobody will believe that we French have ever been destructive to churches. On the other hand look at the deliberate destruction by the Boche of the cathedrals of Rheims and Louvain and all the rest during that war. And, of course, I do not even speak of what the Germans did in the recent war.

"However," said my informant, "when Schweitzer describes the tragic death of his mother who was, as he says, 'run over by cavalry horses' during the same period of fighting, he somehow fails to mention the fact, known to everyone around here, that those mysterious 'cavalry horses' were ridden by *German* soldiers who then occupied the valley."

I began a joint vigil with some French and English newspapermen who had also been stopped by "les roadblocques" and who also knew that Schweitzer would see them if they could make contact directly. At first it wasn't too bad, but after two days of waiting for a glimpse of the doctor, we became restive, bored, and anxious; and I, always prone to visual images, began to fear that we were all like the importunate characters in *The Wizard of Oz* and Kafka's *The Castle,* who had made desperate pilgrimages to seek salvation from the lord of a mythical kingdom—only to find that he really did not exist!

So on the third day I was very relieved to learn that our invisible man did indeed exist: Early that morning he had been seen at a funeral service in a neighboring village. Everyone was talking about "the woman in black" who had appeared at Dr. Schweitzer's door the night before and had "asked to see him." But, as the woman herself told it, she had been given the routine answer: "Dr. Schweitzer cannot see anyone." Then, just as she had turned to leave, Dr. Schweitzer suddenly appeared in the doorway and said to his assistant, angrily, "Who is this 'Dr. Schweitzer' that cannot see anyone?!" and invited her to enter. Tearfully she told him that her husband had just died, that he had known Albert Schweitzer slightly many years before and had often spoken of him. Would the doctor please attend the funeral service? Dr. Schweitzer did more than agree to attend. Deeply moved by the appeal from a stranger on behalf of a man whom he barely remembered, he spent a good part of the night preparing the eulogy he delivered at the morning memorial service.

On the afternoon of the third day Cyril Radcliffe invited me to go with him on a wine-buying trip for the hotel, promising to show me Kaysersberg (where Schweitzer was born) and several other towns associated with him. After photographing them, we made the rounds of wine cellars in Ricquewihr sampling and gravely discussing the merits of the famous wines. They all tasted the same to me, but I pretended to be an expert. My fakery was soon exposed when I (barbarian!) guzzled some wine. The wine merchant seized my arm and put his hand over the glass: "No! No! Not so fast. You are not drinking the oral douche, the Coh-cah Coh-lah! This is the finest white wine in all of France. Here, let me show you how we do it." He raised his glass ceremoniously to his mouth and tilted it so that the level of the wine came to about an eighth of an inch from, but did not actually touch, his lips. Then, with tightly puckered mouth he inhaled sharply and noisily. Between inhalations he explained: "This vaporizes the wine and makes an *explosif* mixture of air and wine. Try it."

But Cyril Radcliffe intervened. "Hold it," he said, "you're new at this. You'd better sit down." I sat down and proposed two toasts. The first toast was dedicated to our two great countries, but the second toast was a frivolous silent appeal to the picture of Bacchus on the wall to help arrange an early meeting with Schweitzer. I inhaled a gusty mixture—and almost fell off my chair. Wine tasted this way has almost the same effect as anesthetic ether and is almost instantly intoxicating to some people.

Soon, after repeated whiffs of aerated wine, I became a little stoned and announced to nobody in particular that, if a "certain party" was too busy to see me, I would instead spend a week—no a month—making a photo essay on the wine industry of Alsace. And it would be dedicated to the convivial Bacchus, who always had plenty of time for everybody. Wheeeee!

The bibulous appeal to Bacchus produced an immediate result. The hotel-room clerk awakened me at 7:00 the very next morning with the newsflash: Schweitzer was due to arrive at the family church at 8:30 a.m. to give a Bach recital for the ladies of Munster who sewed for the children at Lambaréné. While talking with some of them late the night before he had gratefully and impulsively invited them and had sworn them to secrecy. "But as one can see," said the room clerk, "it is no longer a secret. So, if you want to get *near* the place, you'd better get there by eight."

At 8:00 the streets of Gunsbach were already filled with parked and arriving cars, and the little church courtyard was crowded. Inside the rows of benches were packed, and a number of men and women stood in the aisles and at the rear of the church. They were completely silent and waited in reverent attitudes, some with hands clasped prayerfully. A colleague who had saved a strategic spot near the door for "the press" said that several of those present had driven all night from Paris and Lyons (250–350 miles), and a few had come from border towns in Switzerland and Germany. People had been arriving since 6:00.

At precisely 8:30 Dr. Schweitzer entered the church through a side entrance. With him were two women, one of whom I recognized from photographs as his secretary, Madame Martin. The other was Erica Anderson, the photographer, who was also staying at the Hotel of the Storks and was preparing a book and a biographical film about him. The doctor stood silhouetted against the light, looked around at the hushed audience, made a gesture of despair, and then climbed with surprising agility the steep stairs to the organ loft. Soon the little church was flooded with majestic music. Many of the listening faces became quite beautiful, and some people wept as we listened to this 80-year-old man perform the immortal music of his beloved Bach.

But after only two minutes the music suddenly wavered into a discord. Albert Schweitzer stopped playing, stomped down the organ-loft stairs, and stalked angrily through the stunned audience toward the front door.

Many of the audience walked out ahead of him to join the little mob that had stationed itself outside with cameras and autograph albums at the ready. I raced ahead to a strategic position where I could make a shot of the entire scene and then intercept the doctor as he headed for the street to his home.

But, just as I began shooting the hectic scene, Erica Anderson came running across the courtyard toward me. Ignoring all the amateurs and the other professionals who were also photographing Schweitzer as he left the church, she waved her arms madly to block my shot and shouted: "Madame Martin doesn't want you to photograph him. Madame Martin doesn't want you to!"

Her banzai rush was well executed and nicely timed. I lowered my Rolleiflex, gaped at her in astonishment, and then understood at once why I had been denied access to the doctor. But by this time Dr. Schweitzer was approaching so rapidly that there was no time to deal with this flagrant interference. So, after clearly enunciating one of the more indelicate terms of abuse used in our trade against unfair competitors—regardless of their sex—I sidestepped her and walked up to Dr. Schweitzer. He was still quite upset and complained: "All I want to do is play the wonderful music, but they won't let me! They won't let me!"

I moved in fast, and in a mixture of English and German quickly told him my name, the name of the magazine, threw in the fact that it had a circulation of 4 million American readers, and respectfully asked for a few minutes of his valuable time.

Dr. Schweitzer stopped. His apparent distress vanished, and he answered in German in a harassed but patient manner: "An American. Well! You have come a long way to see me. But, I must admit, I really do *not* like these sidewalk assaults. And I definitely do *not* like to be surprised. Why have you not written to inform me that you were coming?"

Caught in the middle of an intrigue that I had only this minute begun to understand, I stammered: "Several letters and cables have been sent to you this week, Herr Doctor, but—but, because you are so very busy, you haven't come to them."

"Perhaps that is so. Perhaps they have already arrived." Then he laughed and said: "What am I going to do with you fellows! Every one of you knows that I cannot say 'no' to a journalist. But you *also* have to earn a living. Yes, I will see you. But first I must join the ladies of Munster at a little breakfast. I am afraid I have disappointed them. Can you come to my house in exactly one hour?"

The success of this long-awaited encounter with Dr. Schweitzer was most gratifying. But after he walked away to be "sidewalk-assaulted" by two newspaper writers, I found that it had left me shaken and faintly giddy. An extraordinary thing had happened: He had stood only three feet away, and his words and reactions, as well as the instant impression of a strikingly handsome man with a commanding yet kindly presence, had come across vividly. But, and this fact was very upsetting, *I had not been able to see his face clearly* because of an "aura effect" that had come between us. (I had experienced such an effect before, first in 1933 in a tiny auditorium in Philadelphia when I saw Martha Graham in a solo performance for the first time. It had happened again in 1947 when I photographed Albert Einstein as he walked sadly out of a Washington congressional-committee hearing on the question of admitting Jewish refugees into British Palestine. And it had manifested itself for the third time at the mere sight of Greta Garbo walking alone on a New York City street. In each of these seismic little encounters, the image of the magical personality had refused to come into visual focus and had danced about, creating that same giddy sense of unreality.) This "aura effect" has been described as "supernatural" by mystics, but it probably results from a self-dramatizing attempt to foist one's highly charged preconceived image of a great public or private hero upon the *actual* person when he is seen at close range. At such moments the colliding disparate images simply refuse to coincide—and create the discombobulation.

Exactly one hour later a middle-aged woman (a member of his nursing staff?) admitted me to his house: "Ah, yes, the doctor is expecting you. Please to come this way." She conducted me to his study at the front of the house. I saw him seated at his desk near a large bay window and was surprised—this day was *loaded* with surprises—to see that the window was curtainless and that two men were standing in the narrow street staring goggle-eyed at the doctor as if he were on display in Macy's window. But the doctor, busily writing, seemed oblivious to their presence.

Dr. Schweitzer looked up, motioned me to a chair near him, greeted me warmly in German, and took my hand in both of his.

There then began the 30-second contest of mutual appraisal that always takes place when a formidable "subject" meets an interviewer or press photographer. The results of the ensuing session are usually determined in this subtle first exchange. This occasion was no exception.

Genuinely impressed and honored to be admitted to his presence, I bowed slightly (as one does when meeting a very eminent person, especially in Europe). We exchanged some small talk about Alsace (beautiful), the weather (ideal), and my ability to speak German (meager). During this cheerful banter ("Dr. Schweitzer is sometimes a great tease") he looked at me in a friendly but searching way, and I countered with my "photographer's stare" of technical observation. The previous "aura effect" had vanished, and I could see him clearly—the outside anyway.

He was an exceptionally photogenic man, and his piercing look of high intelligence and heroic fearlessness reminded me of Michelangelo's *Moses*, whom he resembled in other ways as well. He also resembled the late Walter Huston in his robust masculine charm (Huston would have been perfect in the title role of a drama about Schweitzer). His austere formality and strength were softened by the constant play of his wit, frequently directed at himself, and by his tousled white hair, his scraggly Nietzschean mustache, and the effect of clothing slightly too large for him—an effect caused by the inevitable shrinking that comes in old age. It was a distressing reminder of his mortality.

The clothing, though perfectly "right" for his lofty personality, was anachronistic: a high wing collar with bow tie, a black-linen duster, suitably baggy dark trousers—a neat crease would have been entirely out of character. He was still dressed, as a comparison with early photographs revealed, in the general style of 1913, the year in which he had renounced Europe to take up his totally new life in the jungle. It was the garb of a man who had broken away from the confining German middle class but still wore the uniform in which he had escaped.

His craggy, sculptured face, with its high cheekbones, could be photographed from any angle but looked best (most flattering to him) in profile or when he looked down. But every formal portrait that I had studied had shown him that way: in right or left profile or looking down at an organ or piano keyboard or at a book or manuscript. Why were there so few formal portraits of the man looking directly into the lens of a professional photographer's camera? Did he control the shooting to that extent? Seconds later, while speculating on these questions, I decisively lost our little joust of mutual appraisal.

The instant of defeat came when I noticed, as he looked directly at me, that behind the captivating manner with which he handled me so effortlessly (I felt like a child in his presence) there was *something else*. That *something else* in his eagle-like gaze seemed to be a glint of secret torment or guilt, an admission of unquenchable sorrow. It evoked at once the deeply moving passages in his autobiography in which he tormentedly confesses his "unworthiness" and his yearning to expiate his "sins" by giving himself totally to suffering mankind and to God. But during this lightning-fast shootdown of probing glances I also saw that he was extremely wary and intolerant of trespassers, and that he had caught me peeking voyeuristically through the keyhole of his eye at the inner Schweitzer.

The telltale "look" disappeared. His smile faded too, though it quickly reappeared as he continued to be his jovial and kindly self. But there was no doubt about it: A series of iron doors had already slammed in my face, and I found myself outside Schweitzerville with the realization that, like all the others who had tried and failed, I would never capture a picture of the man inside. Strange images afflict me in moments of crisis. This time my Polaroid unconscious handed me a color snapshot of myself up a creek in French Equatorial Africa—in a canoe with no paddles.

"Well," I thought, "it's probably a rare privilege to be denied by such a great man. I don't blame him for keeping out intruders. But I still have the impressive exterior Schweitzer to photograph. I'll gladly settle for that." Seeking further consolation I recalled the perceptive remarks of Elizabeth Radcliffe: "No one has ever properly photographed the man. Recently Yussef Karsh, you know the one who did the famous picture of Churchill—stayed with us. After he spent the day with the doctor, he came back to the hotel all excited: 'I have captured the true Schweitzer. He is loving! He is cruel! He is a saint! He is the opposite of a saint! And I have it all on film. I have it! I have it!' But," she shrugged, "he didn't have it. Later, when we saw his pictures of the doctor, they were like all the others—flattering." Now I would be able to tell her why.

The doctor said: "Please excuse me for a moment. I must finish checking this document. It must be sent out immediately." As he checked the document and made a few notations on it with his antique fountain pen (I had expected to see him writing with a feather), I surveyed his very orderly desk, on which the neat bundles of papers were not clipped but tied with string. And there right in front of him he had placed my letter and the communiqués from New York! The desk also displayed some manuscripts and a number of copies of his books, all in the German edition. He also had the usual stationery supplies and equipment—and in a corner of the desk a very withered old apple. A tiny memory bell tinkled! It was—yes it was Johann Christoph Friedrich von Schiller, the great German poet-dramatist, who insisted that he was unable to write unless he could smell the rotten apples that he always kept in his desk. Schiller was also an intimate friend of Goethe—and there we were sitting in the house built in 1927 with the money given to Schweitzer when he received the Goethe prize, the highest honor bestowed in the Germanic world.

Meanwhile, outside, the original pair of Schweitzer watchers had been replaced by five others, to whom our motionless figures must have looked like an exhibit in Madame Tussaud's Wax Museum. I waggled my head about, gave them a waxen smile, and touched my ear to reassure them—and perhaps myself—that I was actually alive.

Dr. Schweitzer put aside his document, took up my

letter, and repeated: "Well, then, you fellows have done it again. You know that I am a weak vessel [we laughed at this obvious absurdity] and that I always end up working for you. But I have a great affection for the American people, who have always been most generous to the hospital and very kind to me. So I will gladly cooperate with you.

"But *they*"—his gestures and mimicry indicated the presence of a Sidney Greenstreet-Peter Lorre cabal of paranoid comedians lurking about somewhere in the town—"*they* tell me that your journal, of whose existence I was unaware until today, has sent you here to make a scandal about me." His jocular manner plainly showed that he didn't believe a word of it.

"Herr Doctor, the word 'scandal' has never been associated with the name Schweitzer in America or anywhere else. Surely you must know that. But the possibility intrigues me. What scandal were *they* referring to?"

This answer delighted him. "Touché! Well done! You and I will get along beautifully." He waved a waggish finger at me: "If you haven't heard anything bad about me, *I* certainly won't tell you."

He looked at my letter. "Let me summarize: you want me to 'offer my observations on the present spiritual state of the world' as it is revealed in the letters written to me by people seeking guidance and what I tell them in my answers. These are good questions."

He looked up at me and said wearily, "I can tell you now, privately, that questions such as these, that are constantly being addressed to me by journalists and by so many of my correspondents, are a terrible burden to me."

He then laughed and said, "You know, don't you, that I usually reserve my 'observations' on such 'profound' questions for my own writings?" (I winced at the delicate touch of sarcasm he applied to the word "profound.") He clapped his hands together: "Done! I will give you some answers—but I will do so in writing. I cannot do it any other way. Agreed?"

When he received my instant agreement he consulted my letter again: "Now we come to the photographs you wish to make. This presents problems." He ran his finger down the list and said peevishly: "First of all, I don't wish to be photographed sitting here in my study. Everybody photographs me sitting in my study. Tell me: Why would anybody wish to see me sitting in my study?" When I inadvertently glanced out the window at the people who never took their eyes off him, he caught me at it and became quite angry. He turned and glared at them, and they, quailing before his look, scattered like chickens. Then he turned on me savagely: "I suppose that *you,* sir, are wondering why I sit here in this room and permit myself to be stared at by these—these idle people? And, my dear sir, I suppose you are asking yourself, 'Why doesn't he put curtains on this window or move to another room in this large house where he can have some privacy?' "

He was quite mistaken. Astonished and acutely embarrassed for him, I was thinking compassionately that even a few years ago this truly formidable man would never have allowed such a ridiculous and demeaning situation to occur. "How dreadfully unfair it is," I thought, "to him to be judged by a stranger who sees him only in his declining years!"

He wasn't through. He answered his rhetorical questions: "No! I refuse! I sat in this study in peace and seclusion for many years when no one—no one—This is my study! It will remain exactly as it is!" Then, in another quick change of mood, he picked up my letter again and said quietly and calmly: "I'm really sorry, but I cannot pose for pictures walking in the street. Or visiting the graves of my beloved parents. Or playing the organ. Or talking to my neighbors—or with my staff as they pack medical supplies for the hospital."

He looked me straight in the eye and said: "When you photograph me, Herr Rosenberg, you will photograph *me alone*. Understood?" (Wow! I understood all right. He did indeed occupy stage center all alone and at all times!)

He continued: "I must tell you in honesty that some associates who are preparing a cinema biography to be released after I am gone—and also a book—have already made many of these same pictures. Besides, you must forgive me, but all of this photography takes so much time, and I just don't have it to give."

He was now very sorry for me. "That doesn't leave you very much, does it? Well," he said consolingly, "I will give you some answers to your questions, and we will make some pictures outside in the garden as I work on the last volume of my *Philosophy of Civilization*. That should satisfy your journal and its readers, not so?"

"No, it won't," I thought, but, remembering previous similar situations, I knew that when the time came I would have to try to get more than *that*.

He was now looking at his clock and at his desk calendar: "But," he said, "I won't be able to see you until the 19th at noon. Can you return then? Do you have other work that will keep you in the vicinity for the next few days?"

"Yes, Herr Doctor, I still have many photographs to make. And I am taking a day or so to explore some old towns nearby and visit some museums."

Dr. Schweitzer brightened up. "How fortunate you

are! If I had the time I would go with you and show you Kaysersberg, where I was born, and many other places. Have you been to the Unterlinden Museum at Colmar?"

"No, not yet, but it's on my list."

"Splendid. When you go there you will, of course, see its main attraction—the *Isenheim Altarpiece* by Matthias Grünewald, one of the masterpieces of German art. Do you know the work of Grünewald?"

"Yes, Herr Doctor, but mostly from reproductions. When I worked in Germany after the war, I saw his Karlsruhe *Crucifixion* and an exhibition of Grünewald drawings at the Alte Pinakothek in Munich."

"Well," he said, "I am impressed. An American journalist who knows the work of Grünewald and who has been to the Alte Pinakothek in Munich!" He stared at the empty street for a moment and then said: "I have a good idea. You have come here and asked me all of these questions. In a sense you have put me to a moral test. Now, my friend, I am going to twist things about and put *you* to such a test."

He laughed heartily at his mischievous idea. "Yes! You must go to see the Grünewald *Crucifixion* painting in Colmar and study it. Then, when we meet again, I will, as an old former schoolteacher, ask you to tell me about it." He beamed at me. "What do you think of that?"

Moral test? "Well," I stammered, "I—I'm a very ordinary man—not really worthy of your—"

He fairly leaped at me as he said: "I'll give you a good clue. I have a secret hidden away in the Grünewald *Crucifixion* at Colmar. See if you can find it!"

As he walked me toward the door, he said quite paternally: "Now, you just do as I tell you. I am not only your senior but also a medical doctor. My test will be good for you, and maybe you can mention it for your article."

I was all adither when the doctor's front door closed behind me. Dr. Schweitzer's unusual challenge based on the now-mysterious Grünewald painting left me with mixed emotions. This assignment had started out simply enough: "Ask Schweitzer the questions, make the best possible photographs, and then go on to the next assignment." But the great man had captured my imagination and sent me on a fascinating intellectual treasure hunt. Was this task his way of sharing a painting that had special meaning for him? A parable of some kind? Or was he being grandly mischievous?

I was flattered and grateful at this sudden turn of events. Schweitzer, obviously a great teacher, had added an exciting new whodunit dimension to a painting that I knew quite well from the smaller version at Karlsruhe, from reproductions, and from several critical studies. There was only one drawback to this situation—I really did not wish to study the Grünewald *Crucifixion* at Colmar!

Henry Miller has written, "When you stare at a painting, it stares right back at you." I did not relish the prospect of an eyeball-to-eyeball confrontation with a German crucifixion painting. My reluctance arose from years of experience as an art buff in museums in the United States and Europe, where I had come to admire early German *secular* art and to shun German medieval paintings of the slaughter of martyrs and innocents. The artists were far too clinically precise in their rendition of torture and the gory wounds and bestowed too much loving detail on the hammer and nails, the pincers, the red-hot pokers, the knives, and all the other Hammacher Schlemmer gadgetry of torture. To me their sadism far outweighed their fine artistic qualities and gave the impression, probably mistaken, that the artists and their patrons enjoyed the sadomasochistic exchanges and had missed the point of the symbolic sacrifices of their martyrs.

I preferred the early Flemish or Italian masters, who painted the same scenes of martyrdom but who did so with compassion for the victims and for those who looked on at the painted tragedies. Cimabue, the greatest of the early Italian masters, also painted several Crucifixions (one was destroyed in the recent Florence flood) that are superior to the Grünewald in every respect. Cimabue also reveals the agony of Jesus but surrounds His tortured hands and feet with tiny flowerlike designs that reveal the artist's desire to heal, to use art as prophylaxis.

As I drove to Colmar after lunch, an underlying uneasiness forced its way into soliloquy: "It is too damned soon after Hitler to assimilate such paintings —even Grünewald—in aesthetic terms." I had just revisited Dachau and seen that the death camp, which I had photographed on assignment in 1946, had been turned into a green memorial park and that the old barracks were "off limits." The ashes in the crematorium ovens had been removed and replaced by wreaths and hand-written cards expressing profound sympathy or begging forgiveness. A sign that I had "shot" at its location near the ovens in 1946 had disappeared from the now whitewashed (!) walls. Addressed to Nazi camp personnel it had stated merely, "Cleanliness is next to Godliness." An understandable human attempt to mitigate horror and guilt was in process. Do I, self-appointed judge, approve of this bargain imposed upon the dead by the living? I vacillate, but I think I tend to side with the sincerely repentant living, as nothing will bring back the dead.

But these morbid ramblings may have been instigated in part by the more immediate fear of falling into a journalistic trap. "The world needs great heroes" I warned myself, "and it has wholeheartedly found one in Albert Schweitzer. Later, perhaps, the fickle public will accept or even demand the objective story, the story behind the story, or even the heart-cooling debunk." (I had already heard rumors about the primitive conditions at Lambaréné" and some very vague but disturbing insinuations about Schweitzer's "power motives.") "Yes," I thought, "the appointed hero must suffer and die—over and over and over again in each ritual retelling of his sacrificial adventures."

But on that July afternoon in 1955 a journalist really had only two choices with respect to Schweitzer. He could write a sentimental, eulogistic Reader's Digestible (with sobbing violins in the background) to give the reader a vicarious thrill of identification with the great man who had sacrificed everything, et cetera, et cetera. Or, naïvely presumptuous, he could fall into the error of thinking that he alone had been ordained by fate to separate the "real Schweitzer" from the "mythical Schweitzer." But what if they were one and the same?

I scolded my distorted image in the car's rear-view mirror: "Even if you had the intellect and training—and you haven't—to penetrate the many layers of Schweitzer's personality, it would still take a lifetime free of deadlines to make such a study in depth. Besides, even a fool knows—and if he doesn't his editor will soon tell him—that anyone who even slightly tarnishes the shining image of a mass hero will wind up with his typing finger in a splint and writer's cramp all over. The offended reader will start muttering about Judas or John Wilkes Booth or—

worse—will think of one of those bad guys with a mustache in a western."

You can imagine, then, the mixed feelings with which I entered the Musée Unterlinden (Schweitzer had called it by its German name) and approached the large room that houses the Grünewald altarpiece.

It was a shocker. The little reproductions that I had seen and the smaller version of it at Karlsruhe had not prepared me for this ten-foot greater-than-life-size representation of Calvary. It was like witnessing an actual crucifixion.

It is the middle of the night, and the Roman murderers have long since departed, leaving the dying victim and his four mourners: the Virgin Mary, St. John the Evangelist, Mary Magdalen, and a curiously unmoved St. John the Baptist. This "forerunner" of Jesus was, of course, already dead at the time of the Crucifixion but had been resurrected to point a cartoon-like finger at the man on the cross and say, "He will increase, but I will decrease," a prophecy, biblical scholars agree, of the preordained greatness of Jesus. But the others, still living, are mourning bitterly. The Virgin is prevented from fainting to the ground by the supporting arm of the youthful John the Evangelist. Mary Magdalen is wringing her hands and weeping at the foot of the cross. The larger-than-life crucified Jesus is terrifying to behold. The unique feature of this painting, though, is the fact, well-known to scholars, that Grünewald, after painting all the nail wounds and marks of the scourging inflicted by the Romans—had *added* a great many other wounds and sores of a totally unrelated nature.

Could Schweitzer have been referring to these additional wounds? The critical studies of this well-documented work agreed that Grünewald had been commissioned in 1496 by Guido Guersi, the preceptor of the hospital Order of St. Anthony, to paint a "therapeutic" picture. The Antonine monastic healing order at Isenheim (Alsace) "offered refuge to those afflicted with epilepsy, tetanus, mental disease, gangrene and the new scourge of syphilis, brought back from America by Columbus's men and other early Spanish explorers." As there was no immunity to the last disease at first, Europe was ravaged by it.

New patients at the Isenheim hospital were taken first to the monastery chapel and shown that Jesus had offered to take all the sins of the world upon Himself and now displayed them in symbolic form on His person. Prayers for miraculous recovery (there was little hope of secular cure) were then offered. The picture was intended to be so overwhelming in its effect that patients who saw it would be instantly shocked into normality.

But these medical connections with Schweitzer had to be discounted because his manner had not hinted at such a powerful "secret" meaning. Nevertheless, on reflection the similarities were striking: Dr. Schweitzer was also the "preceptor" of a semimonastic secular hospital in Africa, one that treated all the same diseases (and more). Prayers were also a feature of life at Lambaréné, a medical mission. Also, and this point amused me, Dr. Schweitzer had therapeutically prescribed this painting as "good" for me. What had his sharp diagnostic eye told him about me? I ran my fatigued mind down a hypothetical list of ailments and settled for the dread *aesthete's foot.*

I stared at the unhappy figure of Mary Magdalen. Nothing. Near her I saw an apothecary's jar, dated 1515. Was it Schweitzer's clue? Did it signify that his healing arts were identified with Jesus? No, that couldn't be it. The jar was closed; the fatal injuries were too high to reach its contents were obviously inadequate to the situation. As, still searching for the Schweitzerian needle in a burning haystack, I stared again at Mary Magdalen, I could think only that the word "maudlin," which once meant "weeping," comes from the Old French words *maudelyne* and *madeleine* (Magdalen). The word was coined to describe the manner in which medieval painters like Grünewald always showed Mary Magdalen weeping at the foot of the cross. But Grünewald and Schweitzer tolerated no such frivolous etymological digression, and I now stared—quite fruitlessly—at the figures of the Virgin and the young St. John the Evangelist, who tried vainly to comfort her.

That left only St. John the Baptist. He looked at me, and I looked at him. He pointed to the cross. I looked at the cross and drew a final blank. I found myself, however, feeling grateful to Grünewald for having "resurrected" John the Baptist and for having handed him back his well-known severed head. I remained stubbornly in front of the painting for a few minutes, but it was no use, and I headed abruptly for the exit.

The happy thought about his head, however, did remind me of a story about John the Baptist and his famous severed-head I'd read in Ridolfi's *Lives of the Venetian Painters.* Young Gentile Bellini was hired in 1496 (the same year Grünewald began his *Isenheim Altarpiece*) to be the court painter of Mahomet II. Bellini was happy in his studio in Constantinople until one day, in a fit of gratitude, he presented the Sultan with a freshly-painted picture of the head of John the Baptist on a silver platter. "The Turk praised it highly," writes Ridolfi, "but remarked that the neck projected out too much from the severed head, and as it appeared to the Sovereign that Gentile remained doubtful, by way of showing him the natural effect, he caused a slave to appear before him, whose head he instantly commanded an attendant to strike off, proving to the painter that, when divided, [the neck] immediately drew back." Ridolfi then adds: "Gentile, from the time he beheld the slave decapitated with so little ceremony, was anxious to return to Venice."

Two suspenseful days later I arrived at the doctor's home, where I was told that he would be busy for a few minutes but had left instructions: To save time I could enter the rear garden and arrange things for photography. I set up a tripod with my color camera and a long portrait lens and moved the white garden table to a spot that offered a good background. The noon light was directly overhead, not good for color photography, but it would have to do. When I returned to the house the doctor was waiting and obviously eager to play our game; he began his interrogation as soon as I entered his study.

"You have been to the museum? *Wunderbar!* Now, tell me," he said as I sat down, "who is in the painting *beside* the man on the cross?"

His first question threw me. Like a skillful trial lawyer, he had phrased it to exclude the areas of discussion that he wanted to avoid. I had planned and rehearsed a strategy that would start innocently with the "added wounds" inflicted on Jesus by Grünewald at the request of his medical patrons. This beginning would carry us, I hoped, to the leading question: Was Schweitzer seeking to emulate or to identify himself with Jesus? But obviously he had anticipated me; he knew the implications of the Grünewald painting far better than I did, and with his very first question had nullified my little strategy!

Abandoning my attempts to speak German, I answered in English, "The others in the picture are the Virgin, St. John the Evangelist, Mary Magdalen, and St. John the Baptist." I hesitated.

"Yes, yes. Go on."

"Well, Herr Doctor, since you have implied by your question that your 'secret' excludes the figure of Jesus on the cross—the dominant one of the great painting—which surprises me—then I gather that you do not perhaps—wish to be identified with—"

He smiled at my hesitation. "Excellent. A reasonable deduction from what I said. No, I do not identify myself with Grünewald's crucified Jesus Christ. Or with anyone's Jesus. I only try to be His servant." His gestures prodded me to continue.

I tried to lead back into the strategy that I had worked out: "Does it have to do with the apothecary's jar? At the foot of the cross? That relates to your hospital work in the service of God and man with the hospital Order of St. Anthony here in Alsace?"

"That's ingenious. I see that you know something about the painting's history. But no. Irrelevant."

I was getting nowhere. "I'm sorry but I really have nothing further to report about the other figures in the Grünewald."

He gave me a hint: "What about John the Evangelist? You haven't said anything about him."

"I did notice that, though he is deep in mourning, he has his back to the man on the cross and is trying to comfort the living mother of Jesus. In that respect he reminds me of your expressed obligation to help the living."

Dr. Schweitzer answered sarcastically: "A noble thought. But that's not it. No connection."

I threw up my hands in surrender. "I give up!" He was annoyed and asked me impatiently: "Didn't you notice that St. John's hair was uncombed? That his hair was unkempt?"

When he saw that I had not noticed the uncombed hair of the least important person in the painting and that I obviously didn't know what in hell he was talking about, he said exultantly: "That's it! That's my secret! You have failed my test!" And at my look of total non-comprehension he laughed uproariously.

He consoled me: "Don't feel badly about failing my test. I have given it to others like yourself, and no one has guessed my little secret." He turned and looked out the window and said: "When I was a small boy, I hated to comb my hair, and my beloved mother was always after me. 'Why don't you comb your hair, Albert?' she would say. 'Why don't you comb your hair?' But I was a strong-willed boy and didn't obey. Then one day, when I was about ten, she began again: 'Albert, why don't you comb your hair?' And I answered my dear mother—a minister's wife mind you—'But mother, in the Grünewald painting at Colmar, John the Evangelist has unkempt hair—and so does John the Baptist. If holy saints don't have to comb their hair, why should I?' " He was now far away and visibly moved by his recollection of that moment in childhood.

I was stunned by the story and immediately gawked at his impressive crown of tousled hair. He saw my primitive response and saw that I had gotten the message. Part of it anyway. He laughed at my bewilderment.

But some questions remained unanswered. "Does this mean that you have identified yourself with John the Evangelist all these years?"

He was his foxy, teasing self again. "All these years? That's a very long time. Why do you ask?"

I was groping: "Does this mean that you wish to be regarded as a minor character in the great drama—that you—"

Dr. Schweitzer rose abruptly. "No more. I have told you as much as I can. The rest you will have to find for yourself." He looked at his wall clock. "We have no more time. Now we must make some pictures in the garden."

As we left I walked rapidly ahead and made a couple of shots of him walking on the street. He stopped and said irritably: "This is not our agreement. Please don't do that again."

In the garden he sat at the table and began working on a manuscript that he had brought with him. I then photographed him (as predicted) in right profile, left profile, and looking down at the manuscript. I shot rapidly, going from one camera to the other. He looked up and said: "Why do you work so fast? I have never seen anyone work so fast."

When I answered: "I always work this fast. And I know how pressed you are for time, Herr Doctor," he looked at me kindly and said: "Don't worry about me. An artist needs time for his work" and resumed his writing. I made a few more portraits and then thought that I would test my previous analysis of the Schweitzer photographs that I had seen.

"Excuse me, sir, but would you please look directly into the lens of the camera?" He did so but most grudgingly. I made one more picture, and he said abruptly: "We are finished. No more pictures. You have enough. There are already far too many photographs of me in existence. If people don't know what this face looks like by now. Please come here, if you don't mind. I have a present or two for you."

He then gave me the manuscript that he had been working on. It was not, as I had thought, part of his *Philosophy of Civilization* but the written answers to the questions that the magazine had asked him. "I spent all of last night preparing these answers for your American readers. But for you I have these books. With my compliments."

He brushed aside my thanks for his gift of precious time and thought. "Never mind all that. I enjoyed our little exchange of ideas. If you come by this way again —and I am still here—come talk with me. *Wiedersehen!*"

As he walked away and disappeared around the corner of his home, I continued to ask myself questions: "Was he telling me that he is not a saint upon whom the vicarious sinners of the world should place their burdens? Was he—are we all—only little boys with rumpled hair who are present—"

My surrealist flashback to *The Wizard of Oz* hadn't been so far off, perhaps. We—straw man, cowardly lion, man of tin, and little girl trying to find the way home—had all made the futile pilgrimage to Gunsbach seeking salvation from the lord of a mythical kingdom. But this time the outcome had been different. Dr. Schweitzer had told me that there actually *was* a lord in his kingdom but that it definitely was not Albert Schweitzer.

I felt bereft. We had been given a heart, a brain, some courage, and a few directions for returning home. The rest was up to us.

Never Look Back, Darling!

(THE MYSTERIOUS CASE OF LOT'S WIFE)

FIRST A REVIEW of the facts: Mrs. Lot—she is given no first name in the Old Testament story—is reported to have died in Israel on the 16th of Nisan (March-April), 1898 B.C. The tragedy occurred, the Book of Genesis tells us, while she was fleeing with her husband and two daughters from God's destruction of Sodom. The reported cause of death: instant crystallization into a pillar of sodium chloride. This petrification (or pickling) resulted from her alleged "disobedience" of God's warning not to look back at the fire-and-brimstone holocaust.

My investigation into the events leading up to the moment of her suicidal act tells me that Lot's wife is a very misunderstood woman who has never been given a proper hearing. I believe that the first, nameless Mrs. Lot (that in itself could turn a woman to stone!) was one of the earliest and most tragic victims of the masculine double standard. She has had to endure 3,868 years of censure and ridicule because of the perpetual ignorance, and even suppression, of her story *as it is reported in the Bible.*

My research has so far uncovered the extraordinary fact that *no one* has ever come forward to describe the scandalous *High Noon* melodrama that probably triggered her fatal act. Nor has anyone ever volunteered her side of the strange story. I believe now, on the basis of the facts contained in the biblical story, that the self-destructive action of Lot's wife—if not praiseworthy—was profoundly motivated and deserving of sympathetic attention.

The reason for the conspiracy of silence that has always enveloped this classic episode is simpler than one might imagine: The precise biblical incident that determined the fate of Sodom and of Lot's wife as well was until recently considered of such an "unmentionable" nature that not even scholarly biblical encyclopedias and commentators dared to discuss it. But, fortunately or otherwise, we live in a time when almost anything can be brought into the open for discussion.

The time has come for the first public hearing on the mysterious case of Lot's wife. Such an informal inquest may confirm that her metamorphic death was a just punishment in the context of her time and its moral code. Or it may reveal that her tragic demise was caused by factors other than her alleged "disobedience." A careful study also suggests the strong possibility that Lot's wife was actually the victim of *certain others* who directed and accompanied the party escaping Sodom on that fateful 16th of Nisan.

You may be wondering how I came to be interested in this matter. Well, believe it or not, I was asked to do so by Mrs. Lot herself. I am not the least bit interested in the occult and am not given to mystical visions, but the fact is that the lady has been haunting and nagging me lately. She has never actually *said* anything (her voice box and tongue are petrified, poor dear!), but she has nevertheless made it quite clear that she wants me to tell her story.

Lot's wife first visited me about four months ago while I was browsing in James Joyce's *Ulysses.* I had come to the rowdy scene in a Dublin saloon in which Stephen Dedalus is drinking with a sailor, who sings these lines from an old sea chantey:

> Oh, the bread was harder than brass;
> And the beef was saltier than Lot's wife's arse.

I rarely laugh when reading, but this time I did. Then I wondered if the sailor pronounced the word "brass" as "brarse" to rhyme with "arse." Or did he pronounce "arse" as "ass" to rhyme with "brass?" In a fit of adolescent regression, I repeated the inelegant couplet several times to try the various combinations, and laughed like a loon each time. (It really wasn't *that* funny!)

It was then that Lot's wife appeared. Not as an ectoplasmal form quivering in my rumpus room. Or like the ghost of Hamlet's father. Nothing that glamorous. She arrived in the form of eidetic memory: an uncommonly vivid visual recall of the view from the ancient fortress of Masada in Israel.

Some years ago, as we stood on the historic mesa near the Dead Sea, my guide pointed to a distant tall rock formation, standing all alone on the vast barren plain: "According to legend and history," he said, "*that* is Lot's wife. It's a pity she is so badly eroded that we can't tell which way she is facing. *She* could tell us where to look for Pentapolis, the five lost cities of the plain—Sodom, Gomorrah, Admah, Zeboim, and Zoar. It is that lonely rock standing there that probably inspired the myth of the woman turned to salt and then abandoned."

Now, as I laughed with dumb masculine enjoyment at Joyce's sea chantey, the solitary rock on the Dead Sea plain reappeared. But this time it was different. It was much closer, and the rocks and vegetation on top of the formation had fallen away, revealing a face. Mrs. Lot had turned around and was looking at me very reproachfully.

That look! It was the very same look my mother gave me whenever I did the unpardonable: like deliberately *not* stepping on the newspapers (the Cleveland *Press*) she spread after mopping the floors on Sabbath evenings. It was the long-suffering look she bestowed on her three sons when we stood up on our chairs at suppertime and clownishly sucked up long strands of noodle from the chicken soup. It was her head-shaking expression of despair and lost hope at our exchange of bestial noises with the neighbors' kids.

Yes, Lot's wife was looking at me exactly as my teen-aged girl friends did when I tried that inept funny stuff, and her gaze was like the laser beam of reproach and contempt I get even now (on rare occasions!) from my wife and daughter when the unreconstructed little boy inside shows his Alfred E. Neuman face.

Caught in the misogynistic act, I tried to lie my way out: "Don't look at me that way, Mrs. Lot! It wasn't personal, really it wasn't." This was a feeble defense, so I switched to blush and bluster: "Dammit all, lady! People have been laughing at you for thousands of years. Why pick on *me*?"

Her face became more reproachful than ever at this gauche attack. She faded from view as quickly as she had appeared. But my feeling of guilt persisted. That was no way to treat a lady in distress.

I forgot about this curious reverie until I became aware, in the weeks that followed, that Lot's wife was haunting me. She did so by popping up in almost everything I happened to read or research.

Soon after the fantasy encounter, I glanced at the funnies in the afternoon paper and saw that Charlie Brown in "Peanuts," was pounding blackboard erasers for his teacher. But the other kids made fun of him. Now humiliated, and engulfed in clouds of eraser dust, he was saying forlornly, "I'm turning into a pillar of chalk." (Lot's wife appeared as a faint subliminal image in that one. But she was there all right.)

Shortly after that I read a scene in Herman Melville's first novel, *Typee* (for an essay that I was writing about the author). In it Melville describes his escape from the dreadful *Acushnet.* Melville called the ships that he had sailed on as a youth "wooden-walled Gomorrahs of the deep" because of the rampant homosexuality on board. While they are escaping from the ship the narrator (Melville) says to his companion, "Now, Toby, *not a glance backward* until we stand on the summit of *yonder mountain.*" [my italics]

These words are an almost verbatim copy of the instructions given to the Lot family by the Lord: "*Look not behind thee . . . escape to the mountain,* lest thou be consumed." [my italics]

In another Melville story ("Bartleby the Scrivener") the obsessed narrator asks his weird clerk to assist him in a small matter. When, in his "fluty voice," Bartleby replies, "I prefer not to," the narrator cries out in anguish, "I turned to a pillar of salt!"

On the very next day, while pursuing the question

of Nathaniel Hawthorne's personal influence on Melville (disastrous), I read Hawthorne's story "A Virtuoso Collection." In it the Wandering Jew is showing Hawthorne his collection of profound trivia associated with great events: a swatch of the Golden Fleece, Aladdin's lamp, Peter Stuyvesant's wooden leg, Thomas Jefferson's breeches, the inkstand thrown by Martin Luther at the devil, and the ring sent (in vain) to Queen Elizabeth by Essex, while he was under sentence of death. The undying museum curator also showed Hawthorne the vial of tears in which Niobe, Queen of Thebes, was dissolved. (Remorse and sorrow turned Niobe to stone a few thousand years before, after her boastfulness resulted in the death of her twelve beautiful children.)

Finally, Hawthorne wrote, "I was deeply moved on learning that a shapeless fragment of salt was a relic of that victim of despondency and *sinful regret* —Lot's wife."

(Lot's wife seemed quite agitated as she read this comment over my shoulder. I guess it must have been the great writer's words "sinful regret" that disturbed her. Hawthorne, whose Salem ancestor sentenced Quakers and "witches" to severe and humiliating punishments, was profoundly sympathetic and understanding of errant woman. Was the author of *The Scarlet Letter* implying that Lot's wife was punished for one of the sins of Sodom? Did she commit adultery? Or was she a Lesbian who "looked back" at a lover who was being incinerated?)

Hawthorne's provocative but ambiguous suggestion and my own reaction to the sudden run of coincidental references to the ill-fated woman decided me. I dropped my other research to explore further the mysterious affair of the woman who turned to salt.

The story of Sodom and Gomorrah is a brief digressive interlude within the more important history of the patriarch Abraham, Lot's uncle and protector. (Actually, the Lot family was allowed to escape because of Abraham's influence. Nepotism!) As God is informing Abraham, aged 99, and his rather embarrassed wife Sarah, 90, that a son will be born to them, He suddenly digresses to inform them that he has decided to destroy the "cities of the plain." Horrified, Abraham tries to intercede on behalf of the "righteous" men who will perish with all the wicked. (Nothing at all is said of the innocent children who also lived in the doomed cities.)

There then ensues the famous—and peculiar—haggling scene, in which Jehovah appears to be ill-informed and vacillating, while Abraham, a mere mortal, displays greater compassion, logic, and bargaining skill. He finally persuades God to spare the cities of the plain if only ten good people are found in them.

It seems strange that the writers of this chronicle permitted such an unflattering portrait of the Deity to emerge. It is quite evident from the haggling scene that God, presumably omniscient and omnipresent, known to be aware of "the fall of every sparrow," did not know how many "righteous people" there were in the five cities. This lack of "intelligence" about the condemned people was compounded by the divine comedy of tragic errors that followed.

The capricious and irresolute Deity (it had to be bad writing by the chroniclers!) then reveals his uncertainty—in the manner of all subsequent Chief

Executives. He sent a fact-finding team of angels down to Sodom to look for the required ten good men.

The two angels (disguised as men) arrived at the main gate of Sodom and found Lot—their contact man—waiting for them. He recognized them, bowed low, and brought them to his house as guests. A feast was prepared for them, and Lot ordered a fresh batch of unleavened bread (matzohs) baked. But before the angelic guests retired for the night an astonishing scene of homosexual mass madness took place that immediately decided the fate of Sodom. It is *this* incident, considered carefully, that offers new insight into the alleged "disobedience" of Lot's wife in "turning to look back."

"But before they lay down," Genesis tells us, "the men of the city . . . of Sodom, compassed the house round, both old and young . . . from every quarter." The Bible also tells why: "And they called unto Lot, and said unto him, Where are the men which came into thee this night? bring them out unto us, that we may *know* them." [my italics]

Lot acted quickly—and disastrously—to head off the greatest pederastic gang bang in all recorded history. He shut the door behind him and said, "I pray you, brethren, do not so wickedly. Behold now, I have two daughters which have not known man; let me, I pray you, bring them out unto you, and do ye to them as is good in your eyes; only unto these men do nothing; for therefore came they under the shadow of my roof."

This unbelievable, detestable, blood-curdling and unfatherly act may have been prompted by Lot's fear of God's drastic punishment if the angels were attacked. He also acted in the Old Testament tradition of holy men who (like Abraham) were willing to kill their own children if God ordered it. To be fair, though, it may have been only a delaying action by Lot. He may have guessed, shrewdly, that the queer mob would not be interested in his young daughters but wanted "to know" only the beautiful men inside.

But what did Lot's wife think or say about all this? Obviously she was not consulted and had to stand by helplessly and in terror as her husband offered to throw her daughters to the multitude of sex maniacs huffing and puffing at the door. If she said anything it was probably to suggest to the pious S.O.B. that he offer *himself* to the wolves outside. (When Lot's wife later turned to look back, I believe she may have done so partly to verify to her confused senses that her husband had actually committed such an unforgivable crime against her children and herself.)

When the sex-crazed mob surged up to the door of Lot's house to smash their way in, the angels inside belatedly took action; and, in a masterly pioneering demonstration of mob control, they stopped the onrushing stampede of Sodomites by the ingenious expedient of *blinding* all of them.

The scene that follows this mass blinding is described in the Bible by these simple words: "they wearied themselves to find the door." The magnificent terseness of biblical prose is nowhere more evocative than here. The meagre words suggest an "acting out" of madness and terror that makes any of the recent dramas about the notorious Marquis de Sade look like *Peter Pan.*

They conjure up a picture of many men all suddenly blind but who still continue to grope frantically for the door of Lot's house seeking to rape the angels inside. They cannot find the door. In their frenzy, they collide with one another, cursing and screaming, becoming trampled or killed under the feet of the possessed lunatics behind them. In their confusion they break into other houses and are beaten back with pots and pans in the hands of furious women. Finally, the survivors crawl away from the scene of carnage. Did they remain blind? Were they ever able to find their way home?

These questions become irrelevant in the light of the decision of the besieged, beleaguered, and nearly buggered angels of God, who informed Lot that the city would have to be destroyed and that he and his family must leave immediately.

The rest of the legendary story is fairly well known. God's angels take the escaping quartet by the hand, lead them out of the doomed city, then leave them to find their way to Zoar. God issues his famous order, "Look not behind thee," and proceeds to the genocidal act: "Then the Lord rained upon Sodom and upon Gomorrah brimstone and fire. . . . And he overthrew those cities, and all the plain, and all the inhabitants of the cities, and that which grew upon the ground." And then comes the celebrated passage: "But his wife looked back *from behind him*, and she became a pillar of salt" [my italics]. Nothing more is said about her in the whole Bible. Our last image we have of her—as it has been depicted in thousands of paintings, statues, engravings, and even comic strips—is that of a white statue standing alone on the road from Sodom to Zoar.

Did Lot ever go back to find his wife? To retrieve her, carry her home and stand her in a corner as a parlor decoration? Or, more seriously, did he go back to mourn over her and to bury her? No answers to these questions are given in the Bible.

If no one acted to save her, Lot's wife could have been dissolved in the first winter rains or used as a supply of salt for roving wild animals. A kindly rabbinical legend states that "oxen licked her away each day down to her toes, but each night she was miraculously restored."

Certain aspects of her death are especially puzzling. If the two angels were able to blind an entire multitude to protect *themselves,* why did they not also temporarily blind the Lot family? Then they could have led them by the hand to safety. God had already been apprised of the fatal curiosity of women in the well-known case of Eve, so why did He not, in his omniscience, foresee that his famous order was an incitement to disobedience?

It may be that God knew something about Lot's wife that required such a stratagem for her elimination. In that way he could fulfill his obligation to Abraham to spare his nephew Lot and then execute Lot's wife for the "sin" hinted at by Nathaniel Hawthorne.

You will also have noticed, though, that the biblical account of these desperate refugees says plainly that Lot did not see his wife turn to look back, because she was behind him. Despite the extreme danger of the situation, he walked ahead of her because the rule of that masculine-dominated society required women to walk a few paces behind their lord and master. If in that moment of terror Lot had waived his masculine rights to walk with and protect his wife as they fled from the nuclear-like holocaust, he might have saved her life!

This raises a last, rather startling question: If Lot

did go back, to find his wife, was she *there?* This question arises from the observable fact that *no human* saw what actually happened to Lot's wife. No one saw her turn into a pillar of salt. Her body was never reported found. The information about her death could have come only from the two angelic schlemiels who were the last to see her.

It is quite possible, all things considered, that the humiliated, enraged, and neglected wife of Lot—as she stumbled along alone on the pitch-black road to Zoar behind her husband—suddenly stopped and looked back at the burning city, then returned to Sodom to attempt the rescue of, or to die with, someone else.

After an absence of nearly a month, Lot's wife has just returned to visit me. I have just read her this chapter and carefully studied her stony face all the while. But, like every other woman I have ever known, she has not, by the slightest indication, given me the answers to the many questions raised by my investigations.

In the light of what has already happened to Lot's wife during the past four millennia, I can hardly blame her!

It is my hope, however, that these observations may make all of us better understand those people who dare to look back, even at the peril of their lives, whether they are motivated by "sinful regrets," mere curiosity, or profound compassion.

Come Out, Herman Melville, Wherever You Are!

(THE MAN WHO TURNED TO STONE)

CALL ME SCHLEMIEL. For, on a brutally cold and dismal day in February—when upon the five boroughs of New York City still lay the pretty Medusa snow that crippled our transport, turned us all into disgruntled pillars of snow, and froze the smile on Mayor Lindsay's face—on such a rotten day I crawled into the belly of my little white whale and drove to the Bronx to visit Herman Melville's grave.

It was my third pilgrimage to the wintry site in as many weeks, but that time it was made under the feverish compulsion to take another immediate, long, and hard look at Melville's grave marker. An exciting and strange thing had happened: After years of peering into the translucent but often pitch-black depths of his shifting allegory of the great white whale—and then staring at his tombstone during two recent visits—suddenly a new, previously unrecognized allegory had loomed to the surface.

This new cluster of *deliberately constructed ambiguities* (these words are the key to everything that Melville ever wrote) was consistent with the images he repeated continually until the very end of his life. It also fitted—like an expensive black glove—the well-known facts of his tragic Ishmael life and his blasted career as a writer.

The "new allegory" appeared to have been constructed by Melville himself out of these precise macabre ingredients: his choice of the cemetery he was to be buried in, the mysterious emblems carved on his granite tombstone, and the several meanings of the hieroglyphic white stone itself.

Was this new "thing" merely a phantom mediumistically raised out of an eccentric reading of Herman Melville's highly ambivalent personality, ideas, and imagery? Or had someone finally stumbled upon and recognized the bitter posthumous allegory in stone erected by Melville to mock the world that had contemptuously rejected his printed allegories and sentenced him to a "living death"? Were there other explanations? I was most eager to find out.

My albino Volkswagen approached the Whitestone Bridge with trepidation. On the previous day, its radio reported, strong winds had caused the great structure to sway so badly that motorists had panicked, abandoned their cars on the bridge, and scrambled to the relative safety of the Bronx and Queens. But now the Whitestone was passable.

Soon we were making our way slowly up the icy, snow-engulfed, Bronx River Parkway, and I thought nostalgically of the fine hot summer day in 1952 when I made my very first visit to Melville's burial place.

Curiosity aroused by reading Hart Crane's poem "At Melville's Grave" had led me to Jay Leyda's indispensable *The Melville Log* (1951) and the startling news that America's greatest writer was my neighbor! He was buried in Woodlawn Cemetery, just a few blocks from our apartment.

The same documentary source book revealed that Melville had purchased the lot at Woodlawn many years before his death for his eighteen-year-old son Malcolm, who had been found dead in his room (Melville had to smash down the door) with a bullet wound in his head.

There were, undoubtedly, other motivations for the tragedy, but this distressing question comes to mind: Was the death of the "lovable and obedient" boy connected in some deep emotional way with the recent "self-entombment" of his father? After ten agonizing years of total rejection by publishers and the public because of his inability (or adamant refusal) to write what they wanted, Herman Melville gave up writing professionally to take the menial customs job he held for the rest of his life. "Dollars damn me," he had written to Hawthorne, "and the malicious devil is forever grinning at me, holding the door ajar. . . . What I feel most moved to write, that is banned. Yet . . . write the *other* way I cannot. So the product is a final hash, and all my books are botches." Malcolm Melville shot himself exactly nine months after his father's self-annihilating act.

On my first trip to Woodlawn's office I had been given a printed guide to the mile-square cemetery but had found that Melville's grave was not marked on the map. The whereabouts of Bat Masterson (Bat Masterson! I thought he'd be Out West!), Nelly Bly, F. W. Woolworth, George M. Cohan, Fiorello La Guardia, John ("Bet-a-Million") Gates, Damon Runyon, and many other banking, military, social, commercial, industrial, and show-biz celebrities were clearly indicated—but not that of Herman Melville.

It was sadly obvious that in Woodlawn Cemetery Melville's situation was exactly as it had been during the last 35 years of his life.

When I asked for guidance, Mr. Fred Dapper, Woodlawn's genial chief of security, graciously offered to give me a lift and show me "the highlights of the cemetery." First, in the manner of all good guides, who love to surprise and amaze their tour members, Mr. Dapper drove the entire length of the stone orchard to show me "something very special." When we arrived at the top of its highest hill, he explained: "Woodlawn is located (at this end) in the part of the Bronx known as Gunhill. In October 1776 General Heath's soldiers built a gun redoubt right here where we're standing. Then they pushed their heavy cannon up this hill in the rain and mud —it's all written up in history books—and with their artillery fire covered the famous retreat of General Washington's army from New York to White Plains." (This story struck a Melvillean chord: Melville was very proud of his grandfathers, both heroes of the War of Independence, and, as we shall see, the Gunhill image is one of the most important elements in Melville's "Woodlawn allegory.")

As we drove back and forth through the labyrinth of this huge noncity of 300,000 former people—one of the most interesting places in the United States—we could see how the "rural retreat created in 1863" had been engulfed by New York. Now it is nearly surrounded by dreary orange- and pink-brick apartment buildings, nondescript houses, and untidy industrial yards. But inside its great boulder walls and high iron fences Woodlawn is a beautifully landscaped sanctuary, a surrealist Shangri-la entirely unrelated to the outside world.

The astonishing infrasuburb was filled with enormous, expensive, and impressive mausoleums, palaces, villas, châteaus, mansions, temples, and tombs that began to seem quite familiar after a while. And indeed they were. They had all been copied from famous classical and historic buildings, and soon we gazed in wonder at two Pantheons, three Parthenons, several Roman villas, and any number of well-known Byzantine, Egyptians, Romanesque, Gothic, and Norman edifices—all in reduced scale, of course.

On all sides the hills as far as we could see were covered with mournful cenotaphs, grim sepulchers, alabaster arbors of woe, broken columns signifying premature extinction, and intentionally ruined gazebos of regret. The enthralling, entirely mythicized landscape was filled with these structures set among the larger buildings, and with an equal multitude of marble angels who looked homeward, mourned discreetly, or pointed to heaven with the serene confidence of actors in TV commercials.

But the final dramatic touch was provided by the silent corps of thinly clad, topless, and sometimes nude ladies in bronze and stone, who wept unashamedly on grassy graves; proudly held laurel wreaths over the unsung heroes of home, office, and factory; or who waited and waited, ever-so-patiently, in front of the padlocked rusted iron doors of certain tombs.

It was all very fascinating, but finally the theatrics of the place lost their magic for a moment. It may have been the cumulative effect of the thrifty, dispassionate granite telegrams engraved upon thousands of tombstones that unnerved me. The beguiling façades no longer concealed entirely, and I felt imprisoned inside a *Bronx River Anthology* of petrified despair, trapped in a vast stone metaphor of death. Scared stiff (sorry, Herman Melville!), I looked for the nearest exit.

But my panic vanished as quickly as it had appeared and everything looked just great again. Then the elegant compromise achieved at Woodlawn between reverence for the dearly departed and reverence for the status requirements of the dearly remaining—reminded me of the latest Sam Goldwyn story then going the rounds.

In this apocryphal anecdote Goldwyn visited the famous Forest Lawn Cemetery in North Hollywood. He saw the beautiful Park of Foreverness, devoid of any grim reminders, the deer grazing on the lawns, the splashing fountains, the graceful stone goddesses standing about; then he witnessed a wedding (and maybe a Bar Mitzvah) staged in an outdoor chapel and heard the "world's 25 most immortal tunes" oozing from the hidden Muzak. Impressed, he turned to a friend and said: "You got to hand it to these dead people. They sure know how to live!"

The glittering Goldwyn fantasy was dispelled by my excellent guide, who had stopped his car once again, this time to show me the beautifully designed doors and window gratings on a genuine replica of Hadrian's tomb (about one-eighth the original size). We had already seen similar windows and doors, but these particular ones were decorated with the many birds, beasts, and fish that symbolize resurrection, reincarnation, and eternal life.

The leaping fish reminded me of the Melville insights inadvertently revealed to me by a Vatican scholar, who explained that the earliest Christians were interred in stone sarcophagi decorated with scenes from the Old Testament story of Jonah being swallowed by God's "great fish," or whale, and remaining in its belly for three days and nights before being regurgitated. To the early Christians the Jonah story prefigured the later story of Christ's Resurrection after three days in His tomb.

The priest also explained that the Christian fathers were fascinated by intricate mystical puns and used the "sarcophagus" because the word itself meant "flesh eater" or "flesh swallower"—a parallel to Jonah's whale. Through this deadly serious play on words the burial ritual became an allegorical charade in which the sarcophagus was the belly of a whale or god-like fish where the good Christian confidently awaited rebirth.

Remembering Melville's prodigious use of very serious puns (some poetic, some obscene) and his profound involvement with the Bible and esoteric Christianity, I wondered if he, too, had used this "Whale-as-Christ" association. Several scholarly interpreters of *Moby Dick* had already recognized that Herman had melvilleanously cast his malevolent sea-beast in the image of Jehovah, with Captain Ahab as Lucifer. But the whale as Christ? That seemed far-fetched and impossible! Later, however, I learned that in his near-clairvoyant essay *Moby Dick*, published in 1923, D. H. Lawrence had hinted that Melville's omni-symbolical whale was also a fictional avatar of Jesus Christ.

After this meditation, we continued our pilgrims' progress through Melville's Woodlawn (how he would have enjoyed this trip!) and soon arrived before a full-scale facsimile of the magnificent fifteenth-century château at Amboise. Fred Dapper said respectfully, "August Belmont, the famous banker and sportsman, is buried in there." Then, as if reading my mercenary thoughts, he exclaimed: "You couldn't touch that building today for less than three million dollars! And, if you had the money, where would you find the craftsmen?" He waited briefly for my answer to the vexing problem, but when he sensed that, though I had the three million, I didn't know where to find the craftsmen he let me off the hook: "See that fence off there in the distance? That is where, on the night of March 12, 1932, the kidnapper of the Lindbergh baby, Bruno Richard Hauptmann, hid inside the cemetery and had his meeting with Dr. 'Jafsie' Condon about the ransom money. The poor child was already dead, and he was asking for the money.

"Then Hauptmann saw the approaching lights of one of our night patrol cars, climbed over the fence, and ran off into Van Cortlandt Park over there, with the old fellah—Condon must have been at least 70—right after him. Condon actually caught up with him and tried to get Hauptmann to return the child. But it was too late."

Thinking back to that memorable first visit to Melville's grave at Woodlawn in the company of the warm-hearted Fred Dapper, I believe that it was his sad thoughts about the innocent victim in the Lindbergh tragedy that prompted his next act. He suddenly drove off the main street on which we were traveling and into a side path, stopped his car, and motioned me to follow him. We walked a few feet and stopped before an antebellum Victorian marble statue of a young girl.

I said anxiously: "Herman Melville? Are we anywhere near Mr. Melville's place?"

Fred said: "Sure we are. We'll be there in a jiffy. But I thought you would want to see this memorial put up for the girl who was frightened to death by a mouse."

Now metamorphosed into marble and seriously corroded by acids in the atmosphere, the young stone maiden of about fifteen years, has been sewing but has let her work drop into her lap. Her scissors, perfectly carved in the tiniest detail, has fallen to the floor. She is staring into space and daydreaming, one imagines, of her "first love." At the rear of the ottoman on which she sits, there is a neatly carved mouse hole from which a small mouse is emerging.

As I knelt down on my hands and knees for a close look at the lethal rodent, Fred Dapper said: "The story about her being frightened to death by this little culprit may not be true. I have also been told that the mouse is a symbol of immortality."

(A recent field investigation into house-mouse lore has resulted in a full clearance for the mouse alleged to have frightened the girl to death. Actually, the creature was there on an errand of tender mercy, because the mouse is an emblem of the blessed Gertrude, of Nivelles, patroness of the souls of children and young maidens. A standard *Lives of the Saints* states piously:

> Gertrude is always depicted with several mice climbing up her crozier or playing with her distaff. No satisfactory explanation for this symbolism has been found, but it is popularly supposed that when Gertrude was spinning, the Devil in the form of a mouse gnawed her thread in order to provoke her to lose her temper.

But the unflappable Gertrude passed the Satanic ordeal by thread gnawing with flying colors and was later canonized and appointed manageress of a youth hostel one-third of the way to Heaven. "On their three-day voyage to the Final Judgment, the souls of children and maidens lodge with St. Gertrude on the first night." Who do they stay with on the second night? With St. Michael, dum-dum.)

I found the face of the mouse inscrutable and arose. We went back to the car and soon arrived at the Melville family plot. There my guide and friend shook my hand warmly and left me standing in front of Herman Melville's grave.

Melville's grave and tombstone were, to put it mildly, very disappointing. After the *guignol* extravaganza and monumental trivia of much of Woodlawn, one expected to see an impressively artistic monument worthy of one of the greatest geniuses this country has ever produced. But, like the memorials of his wife, Elizabeth (who survived him by many years); his daughter, Elizabeth; and his two sons, Malcolm and Stanwix, who died young, Melville's tombstone was small, conventional, lower middle-class and executed in the clumsy funerary style of the 1890s.

But, as I looked at it longer, the wrinkled white-granite stone began to seem extraordinary, for it bore no epitaph at all. At its base were the unadorned facts:

HERMAN MELVILLE

August 1, 1819 September 28, 1891

Above this simple statement, on the largest part of the roughhewn druidic stone was carved a large blank scroll and underneath it a quill pen. There was also a thickly carved leafy vine, which "grew" out of the carved earth next to Melville's name. The vine climbed up the stone, passed behind the blank scroll, encircled it, and then mysteriously disappeared into the body of the white stone itself.

Whose idea was this marker? I was at once convinced, because of Melville's noticeable preoccupation with "hieroglyphs" and "hidden secrets" throughout his work, that it was all his own idea. Recently I asked his granddaughter, Mrs. Frances Osborne, who remembers him very vividly, about the matter, and she answered simply: "The tombstone? He wanted it that way!"

Melville once wrote: "Alone in my chamber, in profound silence—as I am now. This silence is a strange thing. No wonder the old Greeks deemed it the vestibule to the higher mysteries." How right he was! At first the dismaying silence and blankness of his scroll evoked only blankness in return. But before long, like everything touched by Melville's genius, the empty scroll and the proffered pen commanded a response: apology, explanation, consolation, as well as literary associations of all kinds. First, some half-remembered lines from Shakespeare that spoke of "vain, inglorious death" and "scrolls." Then a vision of one of the last drawings by Leonardo da Vinci, made when he was very old: a collapsing house of cards with the bitter caption "This was my life." Third, and most vivid, the title page of an "emblematical" book by the Elizabethan Henry Peacham with an engraving of a "hidden author" concealed behind a curtain. Only his forearm protrudes, to write with a feathered pen (just like the one before me) upon a scroll (like the one before me) a mysterious anagram in Latin.

Then more and more images projected themselves on the white granite stone. They were scenes from Melville's life when he, too, had stood before white stones and graves and had tried to fathom the mysteries they concealed. They happened in 1857, when he went to the Holy Land, which he later referred to with loathing as a Terra Damnata, an "accursed land . . . desolated by the fatal embrace of the Deity." On his way home he stopped at Rome where, as an obsessive cemetery buff, he visited the grave of John Keats and read the famous epitaph, which resembles the nonepitaph on his own grave: "Here lies one whose name is writ in water."

His private journal shows that Melville avoided the living in Rome and spent all his days prowling in catacombs, ruins, and museums, where he stood entranced before statues of hundreds and hundreds of Greeks and Romans, once living and now metamorphosed into battered stone, rather like his own frozen self. (After his return home he lectured to audiences as bored stiff as he was about Roman statuary. He was really talking about himself, the Pygmalion story in reverse.)

But Melville had a special favorite among the petrified ancients: He was Antinoüs, the exquisitely beautiful boy "mistress" of Emperor Hadrian. Twice Melville made long trips to see famous busts of Antinoüs and then walked clear across Rome to pay homage at the cenotaph erected by Hadrian for his "lost love." In his private journal Melville recorded this incident with eloquent terseness: "Antinoüs, beautiful.—Walked to the Pincian Hill [the cenotaph of Antinoüs]", and then in a phrase evoking the biblical punishment of death by stoning for "unnatural vices" he added: "Preposterous touring *within a stone's throw* of Antinoüs. *How little influence truth has in the world!*" [my italics].

Melville wrote poems to Antinoüs and created

Billy Budd (written in the last year of his life and found unpublished among his papers), whose title character, created in the exact physical image of Antinoüs, who wears *vines and buds* in his hair. He also surrounded himself in his later years with many mute stone companions. And in his parlor stood a larger-than-life bust of Antinoüs—"covered by Mrs. Melville with a veil to keep off the dust." The beautiful veiled Antinoüs (who frightened at least one of his grandchildren—Mrs. Osborne) remained there until Melville's death in 1891, when he was exiled to the public library of East Orange, New Jersey—and then mysteriously disappeared.

Keats's famous epitaph certainly matches the silent reproach of the Woodlawn monument. Remembering it also recalled to me a poem reprinted in the *Melville Log*. It came from a book of verse written by Thomas Hood and owned by Melville during his "great seclusion." Melville had heavily underscored the following lines:

> What is a poet's fate?
> To write his thoughts upon a slate;—
> The Critic spits on what is done,—
> Gives it a swipe—and all is gone.

Was Melville saying, "Everything I tried to accomplish was spit upon and obliterated by my contemporaries"? Or was he announcing with supreme confidence: "Posterity will judge my work. The just epitaph will be written by future visitors who will make pilgrimages to my grave."

Woodlawn's officials have said that sometimes they find glowing graffiti on Melville's scroll. Occasionally they find that someone has written the stirring first words of *Moby Dick*—"Call me Ishmael"—in appreciation of Melville's Ishmael-like tribulations.

The terse unadorned vital numbers below Herman Melville's name on his tombstone do not reveal, of course, that when he was born (August 1, 1819) his marvelous grandfather Major Thomas Melville was still walking the streets of Boston proudly wearing the old cocked hat of the Revolution. He was, in fact, "one of the legendary band of "Mohawks" who, on the night of December 16, 1773, dumped the British tea into Boston harbor. (Some of the Soochong tea leaves found in Tom Melville's boots after the "tea-in" are still preserved as a family treasure.)

Herman Melville's father, Allan, was a well-educated and successful merchant, who moved his business from New York City, where the future author had been born, to Albany. In 1832, when Herman was twelve, Allan Melville died in bankruptcy and deep emotional distress, leaving his family penniless.

The double trauma of his beloved father's death and rejection by his "haughty and cold" mother (who preferred his brother Gansevoort) decided the course of Herman Melville's life. Because of the general "hard times" and poverty of his family, Herman's education was cut short. After some unrewarding jobs, he was forced by circumstances—and by his questing Ulyssean nature—to seek a new life at sea, first on a trans-Atlantic passenger boat and then on the whaling ship *Acushnet.*

But life aboard the *Acushnet* was brutal, filthy, and degrading. Melville, who later referred to the vessels he sailed on as "wooden-walled Gomorrahs of the Deep," because of their rampant homosexuality, finally jumped ship in the Marquesan harbor of Nukuhiva in the company of a rather effeminate comrade named Toby Greene. The boys found refuge with a "cannibal" tribe; after a mysterious separation from Toby, Melville stayed four weeks and had the "adventures" that formed the basis of his somewhat allegorical *Typee.* But while he was enjoying an idyllic love affair with the native girl who later appeared as the fictional Fayaway, Melville began to suspect that the flesh-eating Marquesans (including Fayaway) were planning a tribal feast in which the tasty grandson of Major Melville would be served up with an apple in his mouth. He made his escape to another ship that turned out to be as bad as the *Acushnet,* eventually returning home as a sailor aboard the frigate *United States.*

Melville quit the sea and decided to write about his South Seas adventures. With the help of his brother Gansevoort, then working in England, he found a publisher for *Typee* and, with remarkable ease, won immediate success in England and then in the United States.

Perhaps he was too lucky. Although *Typee* was moderately successful and made him an "instant author," writing did not provide sufficient income; and Melville tried (unsuccessfully) to find a job in the U.S. Treasury Department in Washington.

But, on the strength of *Typee*'s success, an advance on his next book, and his acceptance in New York literary society, the young author then decided to gamble on a career as a writer. But he made two understandable mistakes, based perhaps on his desire to restore the Melville family status. He fell in love with and married Elizabeth, the daughter of Lemuel Shaw, Chief Justice of the Massachusetts Supreme Court; and, though he knew nothing about farming, he bought a large property in Pittsfield, Massachusetts.

Another eventually catastrophic "mistake" grew

out of the move to Pittsfield. There he met, and, as Somerset Maugham (of all people!) coyly expressed it in his essay on *Moby Dick*, "he developed a 'school-boy' crush on Nathaniel Hawthorne."

The "school-boy crush," if that is what it was, seems to have been of a highly intellectual nature, and it was expressed in a published essay about Hawthorne (written *before* they met). The essay, "Hawthorne and his Mosses," contains metaphors of intense sexual longing that could have been written and published only in that pre-Freudian era.

Before meeting Hawthorne, Melville had been so starved for intellectual companionship that he had fantasized (in a letter) the return to life of his really great "crush"—William Shakespeare. In the manner of lonely children who create imaginary playmates and then play "house," Melville installed the author of *Macbeth, Hamlet,* and *King Lear* in a suite at the Astor Hotel, "left his card," and then "promenaded down Broadway" and drank punch with him. But the jocular fantasy ended on a most self-revealing and agonized note. Removing the "Elizabethan muzzle of fear" from the face of Shakespeare, Melville asked him to reveal the profound secret truths always darkly hinted at in his great dramas and sonnets. Even Melville's jocular fantasies are allegories of his inner torment.

After Melville read *The Scarlet Letter* and other allegorical stories by Hawthorne, he mistakenly believed that he had found the "American Shakespeare"; when he met him, he transferred a bit too much of his passionate feeling for Shakespeare to the account of his silent and reserved neighbor. At first, Hawthorne was flattered by Melville's adulation and exuberant talk, but then he gradually withdrew and chilled the friendship.

Most biographers of the two men believe, however, that before he did so he influenced Melville to change the book then in progress. As a result, *Moby Dick,* begun as another romantic novel of sea adventure, became a lofty Miltonesque allegory of man against God, universe, fate (and only God knows what else) incarnate in the whale.

Melville never recovered from Hawthorne's refusal to meet him on equal emotional terms. Hawthorne soon intensified his rejection, but Melville's one-sided fixation never died, and later was expressed in many curious ways. Hawthorne has been recognized in several of Melville's stories about men who withdraw from life, wither away, or even die when they are badly used or rejected. At the very end of his life, I discovered, Melville used a symbolic representation of Hawthorne as one of the major ingredients of the "Woodlawn allegory in stone."

Melville was in constant financial trouble. His income from his first five books (four were successful) earned him only $1,200 a year, his wife had only a very small income (despite the eminence of her family), and Melville began to go deeply into debt to his publisher. But he was confident that his sixth book—a "romance based on the whaling industry" —would become a great success and solve all his problems.

After two years of extremely exhausting work that did irreparable damage to his psyche and then to his soma (he became almost blind from eyestrain and sometimes wrote for days with his eyes shut), *Moby Dick* was finally finished and sent to England for publication. There it was issued to the public with a key quotation from *Paradise Lost* on its title page: Melville's hint that *Moby Dick* was to be read as a Miltonian allegory. Incidentally, that crucial quotation from Milton's epic account of the conflict between Satan and Jehovah has never appeared on the title page of any American edition of *Moby Dick.*

But the English publisher expurgated eighty examples of "blasphemy," "phallic obscenities" (both "hetero" and "homo"), and "irreverences to the Crown." The circumexcisions included the entire ninety-fifth chapter, "The Cassock," an incredibly sly "pornographic" assault on the sensibilities of Victorian society in 1851. Later restored to the American edition, it ironically describes the "post-mortemizing," or butchery, by the whalers of the 8-foot penis of a black whale. Bentley, the English publisher, objected to the chapter's numerous and obvious phallic puns, especially to Melville's astonishing comparison of the whale's sexual organ to the black cassocks worn by priests of various denominations.

Even today pious readers would find "The Cassock" offensive (if they understood it). What must then have been the reactions of the mid-Victorian Bentley when confronted with such a Gargantuan "practical joke" in an American manuscript? Melville, curiously enough, was most circumspect, even prudish, in his letters to personal friends. But he seemed ignorant of, or indifferent to, the possible disastrous consequences of this and many other deliberate blasphemies, obscenities, and scatalogical puns scattered through all his published stories.

This paradox raises several very important questions about Melville's career. Was he naïve enough to believe that the ordinary reader would not notice his sly game of mocking with obscenity what he believed to be the greater obscenities? Did he imagine, too, that his contemporary critics and other intellectuals would recognize and applaud the arrival in their midst of an American John Milton, Rabelais, Voltaire, Dante, or Goethe—because he made obscene but profound jokes about sacred idols? (In this respect Melville seems a almost identical twin in spirit to James Joyce, that compulsive truth teller and iconoclast, who could be stopped only—temporarily—by boycott. But Joyce was luckier in his choice of century.)

But even after all the most objectionable material had been removed from *Moby Dick,* not a single English reviewer responded to the book's lofty qualities. Despite the bold hint on its title page, none recognized it as another Miltonian "quarrel with God" (the title phrase of Professor Lawrence Thompson's convincing book about Melville), nor did any grasp the magnificent literary achievement of the young American who had in two short years graduated from the intellectual kindergarten as the writer of one of the greatest of all novels. The book was a failure in England.

One hundred years later, in his introduction to *The World's Ten Best Novels* (by Tolstoy, Balzac, Fielding, Jane Austen, Stendhal, Emily Brontë, Flaubert, Dickens, Dostoevsky—and only Melville among Americans), the middlebrow Somerset Maugham (no allegorist he) wrote:

> It is the sinister and gigantic figure of Captain Ahab that pervades the book and gives it its emotional quality. I can think of no creature in fiction that approaches his stature. You must go to the Greek dramatists for anything like the sense of doom with which everything that you are told about him fills you, and to Shakespeare to find beings of such

> terrible power. It is because Herman Melville created him, that notwithstanding all the reservations one may make, *Moby Dick* is a great, a very great book.

A few months after the chilling English reception of the book, *Moby Dick* appeared in the United States—and all hell broke loose. At first the book received some good reviews, but they became steadily more and more hostile until finally the critics slavered and yapped in hydrophobic rage.

The American reviewers opened the pages of Melville's newest book expecting to find another delightful *Typee,* a romantic escapist tale of adventure at sea with perhaps an episode or two of rapturous carefree fornication with exquisite maidens in a South Sea paradise.

But, instead of a sexual *Paradise Regained,* they were given *Paradise Lost, Gargantua and Pantagruel, Oedipus Rex,* Dante's *Inferno,* Sebastian Brant's *Ship of Fools,* all bewilderingly mixed with *King Lear* and Marlowe's *Doctor Faustus*—books recently devoured, assimilated, and used by Melville.

Except for one or two critics—totally without influence—who saw that *Moby Dick* was an allegory amazingly well written, and filled with fascinating characters, the intellectual community professed complete bafflement. It did not know what to make of the story of an American mariner out of Nantucket, an apparent composite of the biblical Ahab, the mythological Perseus, Old Nick, young Lucifer, the Flying Dutchman, the Ancient Mariner, Ichabod Crane, Beelzebub, Uncle Sam, and the Wandering Jew! Not a gentleman among them, except for Uncle Sam, of course, and what was *he* doing in that evil congregation?

Men who could calmly read, enjoy, and repeat (in private) the obscenities of Rabelais or who could unsqueamishly descend into Dante's sometimes pornographic *Inferno,* which allegorized (in part) the evils of Dante's social world, fled like frightened chipmunks from Melville's allegory aimed (in part) at the American society of 1850. And how could they accept the idea that the oil for their lamps and the perfume and corset stays for their ladies were obtained through the murder by harpoon of a surrogate God! Melville was clearly mad!

The extraordinary effect of *Moby Dick*'s blasphemy and pornography upon its readers should be made the basis of a study in group hysteria and aphasia. The prudery and social repression of the period were so much in command that even the most sophisticated critics "blacked out" intellectually and could not evaluate or even mention the actual intentions of the book.

They were totally unprepared for the "berserk account" of the maddened Ahab, who casts a spell upon his crew and forces it to abandon the profitable oil business to join him in a worldwide hunt for the white whale that has torn off his leg. (D. H. Lawrence sided with the whale and wrote indignantly: "The whale was right, too. Should have torn off both legs, and a bit more besides!" Lawrence always knew sexual allegory when he saw it!)

But when some of the astonished reviewers realized—if they got that far—that Captain Ahab was really Satan and that he wanted to harpoon and kill the whale because he insanely mistook him for God Almighty, they slammed the book shut, and never opened it again.

One French literary critic, removed from the puritanical arena in which Melville fought alone in suicidal combat, did recognize the obvious: "Ahab hurls his harpoon at the white whale only because he cannot find God." But in the United States only one critic (Evart Duyckinck) mentioned vaguely that the book had a possible resemblance to *Paradise Lost* or *Faust.* A few praised *Moby Dick* for its splendid writing and gripping drama, but the rest of the predominantly Ivy League critics dismissed the book as "boring," "unreadable," or "lunatic" and implied that the presumptuous "amateur," who boasted that the "whaling ship was my Yale College and my Harvard," had better go back to writing his South Sea romances.

The truth soon became all too clear: The book was a total failure. During the remaining forty years of Herman Melville's life, only about 2,000 copies were sold—an average of 50 a year. But *Uncle Tom's Cabin,* published at exactly the same time (1851), sold more than 2 million copies in many languages during the first three years after its publication.

The commercial failure of his book, as well as its failure to communicate, was disastrous to Melville in every way. All the promises that he had made to himself, to his family, and to the intellectual community now seemed ridiculous. He had been totally rejected.

When we look back at the beating taken by Melville, we tend to put all the blame on the economics of the time and the ignorance and puritanism of his society. We assume that if Melville were alive today he would find and continue to write for the large responsive audience that has been trained by the allegories of Thomas Mann, Franz Kafka, and James Joyce and educated by psychoanalysis and science.

But such speculations are useless. Melville cannot be rescued from his personal dilemma by any Welesian time machine powered by sympathy. *Moby Dick* could have been created only from Melville's experiences aboard a whaling ship in the 1840s as interpreted by his unique nineteenth-century sensibility and intellect.

But there is reason to believe that Melville may have been prone to self-destruction—and that he may have collaborated in his own martyrdom. He hinted at some dreaded personal catastrophe many times in letters that convey a touch of longing for tragedy. He once wrote to Hawthorne: "I am like one of those seeds taken out of an Egyptian tomb which . . . planted in English soil, developed itself, grew to greenness, and then fell to mould. Now I feel that I am come to the inmost leaf of the bulb and that shortly the flower must fall to the mould."

The letter was written when he had *just begun* to write *Moby Dick*. But, according to the psychoanalyst and writer Henry Murray, Melville's running battle with emotional death lasted throughout his life:

> Melville's position in *Mardi* (an earlier work) may be defined in these words: "If I reach my golden haven, may my annihilation be complete!"; in *Moby Dick:* "I see that I shall be annihilated, but against this verdict I shall hurl an everlasting protest!"; in *Pierre:* "I must make up my mind to the inevitability of annihilation."; in 1856, he said to Hawthorne: "I have pretty much made up my mind to be annihilated."; and in 1891, in *Billy Budd:* "I accept my annihilation."

The reader who wishes to learn "what Herman Melville *really* had in mind when he wrote the allegory rejected by his contemporaries" can do it in two ways. He can read the many scholarly books written about *Moby Dick,* and he will find great intellectual stimulation in the poetic and philosophical tributes to Melville by D. H. Lawrence, Charles Olson (my own Melville mentor), Leslie Fiedler, W. H. Auden, Richard Chase, Lawrence Thompson, Henry Murray, James Baird, Lewis Mumford, and others equally perceptive. Or, if he has the necessary Holmesian talent for ferreting out secrets, he can become his own Melville scholar—a fascinating and endless career.

A successful allegory is a work of art—in this instance a literary work—with many levels of meaning because the subject it seeks to interpret has a matching complexity. An allegory is also an intricate game or contest of wits between the writer and the intelligent reader. To be successful it must be profound in content and of high literary merit, of course, so that it will continually reward the reader as he proceeds with the intellectual treasure hunt.

The creator of an allegory must simultaneously conceal and reveal, tease and challenge the reader; he must give up his secrets very grudgingly. The reader, on the other hand, must be very alert to the writer's tricks and skillful enough to spot the clues in this printed paper game.

The game proceeds—in the example of *Moby Dick*—as one picks up the clues dropped by Melville at rapid intervals. These hints are keys and, when used *immediately,* open the portals to what Melville called "the vestibule of the higher mysteries." As we proceed with the Melville game, we shall open a couple of those doors and "see what we shall see."

Melville may have played the allegorical game too cleverly for the readers of his time, taken them too much by surprise; perhaps he did not even make it clear enough that they were supposed to be playing a game. Parents know that, when playing hide-and-seek with a small child, they must learn to hide in such a manner that they can be easily found without insulting the child by being *too* easily found. Every parent knows the consequences of hiding too well—the panic, the tears, the anger of the child! It may be that Melville hid himself and his allegory too damned well.

(This parallel recalls a terrible trauma of my own childhood in Cleveland, Ohio, when my brothers and I played hide-and-seek with a boy named Benny Sachs. Benny was a genius at hiding, and we could never find him. And how he gloated when we finally had to "give up"! One day I persuaded the other kids to go off and leave him in hiding. I never saw him again! Our family moved out of the neighborhood a few days after we played that last game of hide-and-seek. Now from time to time I have a guilty vision of an eight-year-old boy still hiding under a porch, up a tree, or stuck between the narrow space between two buildings waiting and waiting to be found. Come out! Come out, Benny Sachs! For God's sake come out, wherever you are!)

Now, with a warning from one already hooked that the Melville Game may become addictive, you may begin by first reading *Moby Dick* for its entertainment value, as Somerset Maugham advises:

> Fortunately, *Moby Dick* may be read, and read with passionate interest, without a thought of what allegorical significance it may or may not have. I cannot repeat too often that a book is to be read not for instruction or edification but intelligent enjoyment, and if you find that you cannot get this from [*Moby Dick*] you had far better not read it at all.

"Well, men," as the lieutenant always says to his night patrol in those late late films, "you know the dangers. If anyone wants to stay behind, now is your chance. [Pause] Thanks, men. I appreciate your loyalty. Let's go!"

When you read the book for enjoyment, as Maugham wisely suggests, you will notice that it is festooned with biblical, mythological, historical, and archaeological references. (In his book *In the Wake of the Gods,* a study of Melville's conscious use of mythology, H. Bruce Franklin lists more than 500 mythological references in Melville's writing. But merely note these references; do nothing about them. Then, after you have a sense of the entire story, its drama and its characters, begin the book again. This time *stop* whenever you come to a name or an allusion to the Bible or whatever. *These references are the keys* to Melville's allegory—they open the doors to the rooms of his hidden meaning.)

Bypass at first the 75 crucially significant quotations placed by Melville at the beginning of the book. They announce his elaborate game of allegory and clearly inform the reader (who invariably skips them) what his game is. Later, when you return to those 75 quotations over and over again—especially the first 5 from the Bible—you will be amazed to see how carefully he informed his reader *in advance* of what he was up to.

At the beginning of the narrative are the words "Call me Ishmael." Now, unless you have all the biblical, classical, mythological, and historical dictionaries necessary (about 25), you will have to go to the public library. Begin by reading all you can about Ishmael (which means "God hears").

First read the dramatic story of Ishmael in Genesis: the story of how the jealous Sarah and God's commissioners drive Hagar and her infant son into the desert to die. The rejected Ishmael becomes a "wild ass among men," one "whose hand is against every man," as theirs are against him: a total outcast.

This beginning will bring you to the very essence of Melville's hypnotic ability to compel the reader to seek the inevitable implications of his allusions. "Is Ishmael Melville himself?" may be one of your first questions. In order to find out, you will have to read the many biographies of him. I have already expressed the opinion that he was, but remember that Melville wrote about *all* men who are outcasts or who go in search of a father or the truth or . . .

When you resume your reading of *Moby Dick* you will discover that your collateral reading about Ishmael has altogether transformed your sense of the book. (Later in the book Ishmael, the sailor-narrator, fades out and is seldom mentioned again, having been displaced by that cataclysmic odd couple, Captain Ahab and the whale.) Now you are reading on two levels at the same time. You are at the beginning of Melville scholarship.

After weeks or months (depending upon how fanatical you become in your pursuit of symbolic whales) it should become apparent that Melville meant his readers to make "a trackless voyage through the mind" (his phrase), to become, like himself, a Ulysses searching for elusive truth. (The meanings of *Moby Dick*? One of them is the old truism: It is the questing voyage *itself*.)

Soon, after your warm-up with Ishmael and dozens of other themes stated in the early part of *Moby*

Dick, you will be in shape for Captain Ahab, the first great protagonist of the book. The other is, of course, his honor the whale.

Like Ishmael, Captain Ahab is a man punished by God, and the first association is naturally with the nefarious King Ahab of the Old Testament. Easily led by his wife Jezebel, King Ahab established a temple of Baal, where orgiastic fertility rites were celebrated, and thus incurred the well-known wrath of God.

In the illuminating section on Melville in *Love and Death in the American Novel,* Leslie Fiedler has written:

> Melville's convocation of this idolatry is identified with an even more abominable original by Ishmael's reference to "what is darkly set forth in the fifteenth chapter of the First Book of Kings." The biblical text Melville sends the reader to, deals with the rites practiced by the wicked Queen Maacha before a phallic idol, and makes a specific connection between these rites and sodomy: "And he took away all the sodomites out of the land, and removed the idols his fathers had made."

After exploring all the horrendous implications of the biblical name chosen by Herman Melville, including the prophecy uttered by a weirdo named Elijah before the *Pequod* sails—"The dogs will lick the blood . . ." (of Captain Ahab, a definite reference to the fate of the Old Testament Ahab)—you will probably think that you know something about the master of the *Pequod.*

But first follow up the reference when Captain Ahab first appears to the reader (and to his crew): "His whole high, broad form seemed made of solid bronze, and shaped in an unalterable form, like Cellini's cast Perseus."

Once again an allegorical door opens wide with a single reference key, one that provides a typical Melvillean double image, in which the character described has two opposing characteristics simultaneously. After associating Captain Ahab in the strongest possible manner with the wicked King Ahab, a prime offender against the Judeo-Christian Jehovah, Melville offers the very same man as the God-serving heroic son of Zeus, king of the Greek gods. Captain Ahab is linked to Perseus in several ways. First, Perseus slew a sea monster who was about to devour Andromeda. But his most famous heroic and virtuous act was that depicted in the Cellini statue: (to which Captain Ahab is compared) the decapitation of Medusa.

Medusa? The beautiful severed female head, with its writhing phallic snakes instead of hair, is the hermaphroditic gorgon's head that haunts the Melville's most important stories as his symbol of homosexual guilt. She turns men to stone when they gaze at her, even in their fantasies or dreams.

When Ahab (with harpoon) takes on the identity of Perseus standing with knife in hand and holding the Medusa's head, we may suspect that, if Ahab is Perseus, then the whale may be Medusa. But then where in *Moby Dick* is she to be found?

Melville's Medusa is found first in the tortured soliloquy of Starbuck, who clearly identifies the Medusa: "The white whale is their [the crew's] demigorgon." Then there are two extraordinary scenes peopled by stone men resembling those painted by René Magritte or the "living statues" in the fairy-tale films of Jean Cocteau. They reveal that Ahab's men have been turned to stone because they have seen the Medusa's head in the whale or because they *wish* to see the Medusa's head.

In the first of these scenes the men are those who stand perpetual watch on the masthead, looking out for whales. They are compared, first, to the men who once stood atop the Tower of Babel (punished by God), second, to the sentinels atop the pyramids (where, according to Melville, the "idea" of the "terrible Jehovah" was born), and third, George Washington, Napoleon Bonaparte, and Lord Horatio Nelson (all three "turned to stone" and standing on their granite pillars in Baltimore, Paris, and London!).

But the men who look out for "Medusa whales" are not the only ones transformed into "stone men." One hundred feet below, the rat-infested forecastle becomes, through the fairy-wand of Melvillean metaphor, an underground crypt in whose "triangular oaken vaults" (hammocks!) the snoring men lie like stone effigies of "kings and counsellors" in "chiselled muteness."

Ahab! Perseus! Who next? After putting on these masks and changing them about, Captain Ahab assumes the mask that he wears through most of *Moby Dick:* that of a nineteenth-century successor to John Milton's Lucifer; the whale, of course, fulfills the Miltonian conception of Jehovah. But the author never stops his teasing game with the reader: He hints strangely, deviously, sardonically that the mad captain *might* also be St. George, Vishnu, several Persian gods of good and evil, and even Prometheus, the darling of the Romantic poets and artists of the early nineteenth century. (Sometimes the whale reminds me of Frankenstein's monster. Melville read *Frankenstein* before writing *Moby Dick.*)

But before you choose your favorites from among these masks you may discover, as the poet and the best of Melvilleans, the late Charles Olson did in *Call*

Me Ishmael, that Ahab also wears a "crucifixion" in his face. Now the mask begins to resemble Christ, and Olson has noted that Ahab soliloquizes: "Is then this crown too heavy? This Iron Crown of Lombardy I wear?" The "Iron Crown of Lombardy" supposedly contained a nail once used to pierce the flesh of Christ on the cross.

Herman Melville himself "turned to stone" sometime during the year 1851–1852. He did so, according to my psycholithic drill-core samples, during the writing of his half-deranged superrational novel *Pierre; or the Ambiguities,* the book that he began in desperation while the critics were still violently attacking *Moby Dick.*

The tip-off to the exact moment of emotional petrifaction (or deep freezing) is the punning title of the book. *Pierre* is French for Peter, of course, and also means "rock." The pun was borrowed by Melville from Jesus himself, who made the famous play on words when he said of Peter (Petrus) that he would build his church upon that rock. Everyone present knew exactly what Jesus meant. The always ironic Melville used the pun differently!

Many of his biographers agree that Melville created "Pierre the ambiguous" as a self-portrait during one of the worst years of his life. After the book appeared and met an even worse fate than *Moby Dick,* Melville's uncle and friend Peter Gansevoort said despairingly, "Ah, Herman, Herman, Herman, *thou* art truly ambiguous!"

In this frantic, self-dramatizing confessional, Pierre is the author of "acrostics and anagrams," a sarcastic reference by Melville to his earlier and still undeciphered works. While working on a "sinful book," later self-denounced as a "forgery," Pierre, whom

Henry Murray describes in Miltonian terms as "An American Fallen and Crucified Angel," falls asleep in his chair.

He dreams that, after committing the unpardonable sins of blasphemy, patricide, and incest, he is walking in an infernal haunted landscape, where he comes upon a vast assemblage of stones, which he recognizes as the metamorphosed, mutilated, and petrified corpse of the God-defying Enceladus, a mythological character. In this nightmare the guilt-ridden Pierre identifies himself completely with the divinely-punished Enceladus and fulfills the meaning of his name by "turning to stone":

> Enceladus! It is Enceladus! That moment the phantom faced him; and Pierre saw Enceladus no more; but on the Titan's armless trunk his own duplicate face and features magnifiedly gleamed upon him with *prophetic* discomfiture and woe. With trembling frame he started up from his chair, and *awoke from an ideal horror to his actual grief.* [my emphasis]

Later Pierre sees that his half-sister Isabel, with whom he is living incestuously, resembles the severed head of Medusa. At the end of the book he dies in a stone dungeon whose walls are described as if they were the faces of human beings turned to stone: "Pierre's immortal, immovable bleached cheek was dry; but the stone cheeks of the walls were trickling."

Was Melville aware of what had happened within him? Here is how he describes Pierre after the gigantic crystallization: "As a statue, planted on a revolving pedestal, shows now this limb, now that; now front, now back, now side; continually changing, too, its general profile; *so does the pivoted, statued soul of man, when turned by the hand of Truth."* [my emphasis]

In 1857, the year in which the last of Melville's unsuccessful books (*The Confidence Man*) was published, his family realized that he was undergoing a great crisis of self-flagellation and sent him on a futile therapeutic voyage to the Holy Land. His loved ones knew what had happened and hoped that at the sacred shrines he would hold a summit meeting with the deities whom he had offended and would seek reconciliation and forgiveness.

But his wife and father-in-law (who paid for the trip) did not know how irreversible Herman's condition had become. Melville went to his Terra Damnata determined to ignore their strategy; he made the long sea voyage only to revisit the scenes of his metaphorical transgressions.

In Palestine, according to Charles Olson, Melville became almost insanely obsessed with the death imagery that he saw in the stones of Palestine. In his private journal he wrote notes intended only for himself:

> Barrenness of Judea . . . white mildew pervading whole tracts of landscape—bleached leprosy—encrustations of curses, bones of rocks,—crunched, gnawed, mumbled—mere refuse and rubbish of creation. We read a great deal about stones in the Bible. Monuments and memorials are set up of stones; men are stoned to death; the figurative seed falls in stony places.
>
> Judea is one accumulation of stones—stony mountains and stony plains: stony torrents and stony roads; stony vales & stony fields; stony homes and stony tombs (effaced: stony eyes and stony hearts): stones to the right and stones to the left.

Then, after walking about with his head down most of the time and looking only at stones, Melville visited the reputed site of the destroyed city of Sodom. There, after comparing the salt-encrusted pebbles on the beach to the frothing mouth of a mad dog, he actually drank a little water from the Dead Sea!

Melville's private notes (found after his death) continue: "Bitter is it to be poor & reviled, & Oh, how bitter are these waters of Death, thought I—nought to eat but bitumen ashes (from the incinerated Sodom)—and with dessert of Sodom apples washed down with water from the Dead Sea." Later, after observing that all Palestine, once called "the land of milk and honey," had been reduced to a "skeleton made of bones of rocks," Melville projected himself onto the landscape (as he had projected himself once before onto the stony image of Enceladus) and uttered his anguished cry of recognition: "Is this desolation of the land the result of the fatal embrace of the Deity?"

At the scene of his crime Melville had suddenly seen himself as a man turned to stone by the crushing embrace of the Deity whom he had recently tried to kill in *Moby Dick.*

The Bronx River Parkway had been cleared all the way to 233rd Street, but there we fell behind a big snowplow that soon cleared the short road leading to the main gate of Woodlawn, where we found that all the streets inside the cemetery had been cleared! The dead, with no errands to perform, were doing better than the living.

Soon, standing before the snow-covered grave—for

the third time in a few weeks—I took out the notebook containing the chain of evidence that I hoped would prove that Melville had created a posthumous allegory here at Woodlawn. His choice of cemetery, the symbols carved on the granite, and the several meanings of the white stone itself were his ingredients.

I had delayed my final inspection of the suggested Woodlawn allegory until the most important question had been answered: Had Melville continued captive to his cemetery-graves-petrifaction image until the very end of his life? The answer, after a strenuous search among his privately published poems and personal letters written during "the great silence," seemed to be affirmative. The obsession with guilt and expiation had never left him.

During the year in which Melville became a customs employee, he published a book of about seventy poems on the American Civil War. (His alarmed wife wrote to her mother: "Herman has taken to writing poetry, but don't say anything about it. You know how these things get around!") Most of the poems were on the theme of heroic warriors killed in a noble cause but now forgotten in untended graves. Sixteen of these very empathetic poems were written either in the form of epitaphs or about graves without epitaphs. One, for example, is called "An Uninscribed Monument on a Field in Georgia" and begins:

> No trophy this, a stone unhewn
> The nameless brave, outcast they sleep.

As always with Melville, the poems are self-directed.

Even as early as 1855, the Melville's curious stone-syndrome was expressed in a dedication to the Bunker Hill monument. This dedication prefaced the novel *Israel Potter,* about a Revolutionary War soldier who had been exiled for forty years and then denied a pension when he finally returned to the United States.

The epitaph was addressed directly to the stone monument (previously he had dedicated a book to a stone mountain) in words prophetic of Melville's own burial—not on Bunker Hill but on another Revolutionary battleground, Woodlawn's Gunhill: "Israel Potter well merits the present tribute—a private of Bunker Hill who was years ago promoted to a deeper privacy underground, with the posthumous pension, annually paid him in ever-new mosses and swards."

The last solid link in the chain of evidence was a manuscript fragment found among Melville's papers after his death. The fragment was entitled *Daniel Orme* and is definitely known to have been written during the last year of Melville's life.

This final link was suggested to me by *Herman Melville: A Critical Study,* in which Richard Chase has written:

> The prose sketch labelled "Omitted of Billy Budd" I take to be very much a self-portrait of Herman Melville. It begins by warning the would-be biographer that the face of Daniel Orme is stubbornly visored:
>
> "We try to ascertain from somebody [wrote Melville] the career and experience of the man or seek to obtain this information from the man himself. But what we hear from others may prove to be unreliable gossip, and he himself if approached is fastidiously uncommunicative.
>
> "In short, *he turns out to be like a meteoric stone in a field.* There it is. The neighbors have their say about it, and an odd-enough say it may prove. But what is it? Whence did it come?"

Once again, after a leap in time of forty years from *Moby Dick* and *Pierre,* Melville describes a man as a stone! In this retrospective self-portrait Orme-Melville appears precisely as Melville bitterly conceived himself: a meteoric writer who flashed for a moment and then "burned out" to fall as a stone to lie in a grassy field (in Woodlawn). There people (like me) come and look at the stone and ask unanswerable questions of it. The stone is Melville himself.

Daniel ("God judges") Orme (Scandinavian for "mariner") is a mysteriously solitary and silent old sailor who "slipped into obscure moorings ashore" many years ago. He has been (like Melville) a foretopman on naval ships and is now feared as a *Man forbid*, "one branded by the Evil Spirit"; he wears an agonized look "construed as a self-condemnation for some dark deed of the past."

> One fine Easter Day . . . [Melville wrote,] Orme was found alone and dead on a height overlooking the sea . . . it was a terraced height [Woodlawn], destined for use in war [Gunhill], but in peace offering a sanctuary for anybody [Woodlawn again]. Mounted on it was an obsolete battery of ancient guns [Gunhill again]. Against one of these he was found leaning with his eyes open wide.

Yes, the white granite stone was a "meteoric" stone (Orme-Melville) found lying in a field. But what is it staring at so hard with its metaphorical wide-open eyes?

I telephoned a Woodlawn official, Charles D'Ogostino and asked him, "Which way is Herman Melville facing?" The witty D'Ogostino ("Call me Charley") answered: "Straight up. Looking to heaven. I guess you meant to ask, which way is his gravestone facing? Well, if you stood him up he would be facing north-east."

Northeast. Now, standing at Melville's grave *we* face northeast. What do we see from this hill? Far more important, what did Herman Melville see when he chose this site in 1867, the year after he had abdicated his genius to work in a menial job at the customs house?

At his right he saw the ports of New Bedford and Nantucket, from which he had sailed as Ishmael on the catastrophic hunt for *Moby Dick.* Farther up the coast was Boston, where his grandfather Thomas Melville had poured the tea into Boston harbor. Above Boston in Salem, Massachusetts, was Hawthorne interred four years before (1863). To his left Melville saw Albany, New York, where his father had died bankrupt and in great emotional distress (the unscientific description that his own society used was "raving mad"). Looking northward to Albany he envisaged the city where his frigid mother had refused him love, and where he had been humiliated by menial jobs, and from which he had finally escaped to sea.

In the very center of this biopanorama Melville saw Pittsfield, where he had gone almost blind writing *Moby Dick.* Near Pittsfield was the former home of Nathaniel Hawthorne, upon whom he had called many times, whom he loved in his own highly ambivalent way, and to whom he had written poems of sexual longing. Straight before him was thus the scene of his greatest emotional rejection.

Seen in this total context, the landscape of his life, lying beyond White Plains—and other cities of the plain—suggested a possible interpretation of Melville's white tombstone: a pillar of salt facing back toward his lifetime of real and fantasized tragedy.

When we turn our own eyes away from the panorama of the remembered past to Melville's "granitized" self, we seek the meaning of the carved vine that emerges from the granite earth next to Melville's name, to encircle the blank scroll and then disappear into the stone itself. This vine is the symbol of Nathaniel Hawthorne. Henry Murray has said in his psychoanalytic study of Pierre as Melville: "In *Clarel* [the poem privately printed by Melville after Hawthorne's death] [The character] Vine is unmistakably Hawthorne." Melville biographer Newton Arvin agrees: "Vine is Hawthorne to the life." And William Ellery Sedgewick also concurs: "I am convinced that for Vine Melville drew on his impressions of Hawthorne." Richard Chase adds: "The name 'Vine' is significant of the man's character. He seems to be growing close to the earth and in shadowed places."

In *Clarel* (1876), the five hundred-page poem about Melville's disillusioning voyage to the Holy Land, Vine is Clarel's traveling companion. Chase describes a scene between the two men: Clarel has a "thrill of personal longing" for Vine, and, as the company approaches the ancient city of Sodom, he ventures an uncertain declaration of love, making known a "feminine . . . passionate desire" to call Vine "brother." Vine quickly repulses Clarel with an "inarticulate dark frown."

But this curious metaphor of fertility may also be found in an essay that Melville wrote *before* he met Hawthorne: "Hawthorne and his Mosses." After reading *Mosses from an Old Manse*, Melville had waxed ecstatic: "how magically stole over me this Mossy Man! . . . The soft ravishments of the man spun me around about in a web of dreams."

Then the precise image of Melville as the earth, out of which grows a vine comes from the amazingly sexual "soul" image in the same essay: "I feel that this

Hawthorne has dropped germinous seeds into my soul. He expands and deepens down, the more I contemplate him; and further and further, shoots his strong New England roots into the hot soil in my Southern soul." (Melville signed the essay "By a Virginian Spending July in Vermont.")

The image of Hawthorne as a vine appears again in Melville's well-known poem written after Hawthorne's death in 1863:

Monody

To have known him, to have loved him after loneless
    long;
And then to be estranged in life,
    And neither in the wrong!
And now for death to set his seal—
    Ease me, a little ease, my song! . . .

Beneath the fir-tree crape
    Glazed new with ice *the cloistral vine*
That hid the shyest grape [my emphasis].

And now we come to the final meaning of the hieroglyphic white tombstone itself. I had suspected all along, as I worked out the meanings of the stone (symbolizing, first, Melville himself, the rejected writer offering himself as a scroll upon which future generations might inscribe his greatness, and, second, a man turned to a pillar of rock salt, man of stone through homosexual guilt) that it also had other meanings.

As we have seen, Melville anticipated Freud, understanding and writing his characters with shifting identities and highly ambivalent. That is why Ahab assumes numerous identities—he is *all* men, as everyman is *all* men. But Melville went farther; pantheistically he turned his men into inanimate objects or into animals whenever they seemed to perform that way.

More to the point, I had noticed that *Moby Dick* contains a large number of scattered references to the whale as an ancient fossil, as a rocky promontory (the English title page of the book quotes Milton's image of the Leviathan as the "promontory" or island of the entire world). Melville also describes the whale as a "rock lying in a field," as an "indispensable decoration for a garden like a cupola or monument," and as a stony skeleton used as a temple and covered with hieroglyphics. So I began to suspect that Melville had also made of his own white tombstone a multiple allegory, that it was also intended as a white (granite) whale.

After stating the mystery in his most mischievous manner ("Genius in the Sperm Whale? Has the Sperm Whale ever written a book? No, his great genius is declared . . . in his pyramidal silence," likening the whale to a tomb of the pharaohs), Melville slaps the reader on both cheeks with his challenge:

> Champollion deciphered the wrinkled granite hieroglyphics [*Rosetta Stone*]. But there is no Champollion to decipher the Egypt of every man's face and being. If then Sir William Jones could not read the simplest peasant's face in its profounder and more subtle meanings, he may understand unlettered Ishmael's hope of reading the awful Chaldee of the Sperm Whale's brow. Read it if you can.

My next clue to the identification of Melville's stone as a whale was the following passage:

> My retentive memory of the hieroglyphics of one sperm whale in particular. By its resemblance to . . . the famous hieroglyphic palisades on the banks of the Upper Mississippi. Like those mystic rocks the mystic-marked whale remains undecipherable.
>
> I would say that those New England rocks on the seacoast resemble the Sperm Whale.

Then, after discovering images of ancient fossilized whales or whale skeletons lying in fields of grass strewn through *Moby Dick,* I found that Melville had also included the image of *a man concealed behind a whale that is mistaken for a rock.* Melville quotes from Captain Cook's journal: "In the afternoon we saw what was supposed to be a rock, but it was found to be a dead whale which some Asiatics had killed and were then towing ashore. They seemed to conceal themselves behind the whale to avoid being seen by us."

In adding up the images thus far, we find a mysterious rock or whale lying in a field (like Melville's tombstone) with someone concealed behind it.

The following passage from *Moby Dick* tells us that inside the head of the whale there is a coffin or casket: "The whale's brain is at least twenty feet away from his apparent forehead in life; it is hidden away behind the vast outworks, like the innermost citadel within the fortifications of Quebec. *So like a casket* is it secreted in him" [my italics].

But the ultimate image that we have been seeking —the image of death and resurrection in the whale— is contained in the remarkable scene in *Moby Dick* in which Tashtego falls into the head of the whale (where the finest oil is found) and is drowning until Queequegg dives into the oil and rescues him by means of a Caesarean operation upon the whale. He cuts his way out with his knife and pulls Tashtego after him: "Now had Tashtego perished in that head, it had been a very precious perishing . . . cofined, hearsed and tombed in the secret inner chamber and sanctum sanctorum of the whale."

And that, dear reader, is where Herman Melville lies in Woodlawn Cemetery—within the allegory that he created for himself there. He is "coffined, hearsed and tombed in the secret inner chamber and sanctum sanctorum" of the white whale of god.

The coffin in which he rests is the stone "sarcophagus," or tomb, or whale, or godlike fish inside which Melville, the former antagonist of God now secretly reconciled (perhaps), lies awaiting his resurrection—like Jonah or any good Christian.

Is the resurrection of Herman Melville as a great allegorist now upon us? It appears so. But, while we wait to find out for sure, let's read what Melville himself had to say about his present situation. He wrote to his brother Tom:

> Think of those sensible and sociable millions of fellows all taking a friendly snooze together under the sod; no quarrelling, no imaginary grievances, no envies, no heartburnings, & thinking how much better the other fellow is. None of this: but all equally free-&-easy, they sleep and reel off their nine knots an hour, in perfect amity.

SEX PSYCHE ETCETERA IN THE FILM

PARKER TYLER

A review of the roles of sex and the human psyche in the history of the film. Looking back over the last fifty years, Parker Tyler shows that the bane of the films has been the belief that their true function is the representation of physical reality—the reportorial rather than the artistic view of the world. And too often the sex goddesses of the silver screen rise from foam rubber rather than from a sea of flesh. Focusing on the cinema's use of sex, Tyler surveys the work of directors from Eisenstein and Chaplin to Fellini and Warhol as he discusses sex ritual in film, the modern psyche in film, the film artist in crisis, and the pros and cons of film aesthetics. A poet and writer on art as well as one of America's most influential film critics, Parker Tyler reveals in this volume the profound intuitions and unfailing plastic acumen he brings to his judgments of both form and meaning in film. "Parker Tyler sees, hears, and feels more than any of us."—Richard McLaughlin in the *New York Post*

MEMOIRS OF SHERLOCK HOLMES

SIR ARTHUR CONAN DOYLE

Holmes is in top form for these eleven sinister, brain-twisting cases. Includes such chillers as "Silver Blaze," "The Yellow Face," "The Musgrave Ritual," "The Crooked Man," and "The Final Problem," by which Conan Doyle originally intended to close his famous detective's career.

EPHRAIM KISHON

LOOK BACK, MRS. LOT

An hilarious venture into modern Israel, with the author as both our guide . . . and a participant in the madcap escapades he records. Ephraim Kishon is Israel's top humorist, and this is his first book to be published in English. From the very first page, the Zionist filter is whipped off the lens, and the land flowing with milk and honey lies before our dazzled eyes. A land of muddles and miracles, where anything can happen . . . where the party is the ladder to success . . . where they're determined to rebuild the Tower of Babel.

UNFAIR TO GOLIATH

More hilarious stories of life in modern Israel. In these fun-filled pages, Ephraim Kishon is just as witty about Jewish traffic cops and Israeli plumbing as he is about people who cough at concerts, give you things you can't repay, and make you feel bad just for being alive.